IT'S A MIRACLE!

Jessica Christ, Book 3

H. CLAIRE TAYLOR

Copyright © 2017 by H. Claire Taylor

All rights reserved.

No part of this book may be reproduced in any form or by any electronic or mechanical means, including information storage and retrieval systems, without written permission from the author, except for the use of brief quotations in a book review.

ISBN: 978-0-9996050-2-8 (H. Claire Taylor)

contact@hclairetaylor.com

FFS Media, LLC

Thanks be to Michael Anderle, who helped me spread the gospel, and to Alyssa Archer, who helped me make sure the gospel didn't suck.

And, of course, the Almighty Comedian, who seems stretched a little thin these days.

Contents

Chapter 1	1
Chapter 2	9
Chapter 3	25
Chapter 4	46
Chapter 5	57
Chapter 6	65
Chapter 7	79
Chapter 8	100
Chapter 9	116
Chapter 10	126
Chapter 11	136
Chapter 12	151
Chapter 13	169
Chapter 14	195
Chapter 15	212
Chapter 16	224
Chapter 17	233
Chapter 18	258
Grab a free read	269
Bonus: Nu Alpha Omega	271
About the Author	283
Also by H. Claire Taylor	285

Chapter One

AGC 16

Midway through dragging the straightening iron down a chunk of her ash brown hair, Jessica McCloud paused to focus on the voice coming through the television in the living room. She recognized the speaker instinctively, despite how long it'd been since she'd last spoken with him in person. Maybe that had to do with the fact that it was one of the first voices she'd ever heard. Maybe that was why it was lodged in the recesses of her mind like a piece of spinach between unbrushed teeth.

A rancid burning smell reminded her of what she was doing. "Shit!" She pulled the iron the rest of the way down the strand and then dodged out of the bathroom and into the dim living room.

The first thing her eyes landed upon, though, was Destinee and Coach Rex on the couch, his arm slung over the back and around her mother's shoulder, both sets of eyes glued to the television, their after-dinner Dos Equis still nearly full, sweating and forgotten on the TV tray in front of them.

"What's *he* doing on the news?" asked Jessica, positioning herself next to the couch to get a better look.

Destinee shushed her. "Just watch."

Jimmy's face smiled back from the TV. His teeth looked whiter since the last time she'd seen him, and she suspected that was from no lack of effort on his part. With the money he was pulling in now from his religious endeavors, he could afford the best teeth whitening Midland had to offer, she was sure. His hair, though, looked just the same, slicked back into a perfectly gelled swoop that never moved but somehow also looked natural and like it'd been styled by the hand of God Himself. Of course Jessica knew for certain that wasn't the case.

"... And so it seemed there was really only one thing that I, a humble servant of the Lord, could do to put the God back in government."

"Put the God back in government?" Jessica echoed. "I thought He was never supposed to be there in the first—"

"Shh!" Destinee hissed. "Listen."

"So on this glorious Texas day in May, before all of you, many of whom have been loyal members of the White Light congregation for years, I'm officially announcing my candidacy for Mayor of Midland, the greatest city in the greatest state in the greatest country of the world. No questions please. Thank you." And just like that, Jessica felt nauseated.

Jimmy was making a play—there was no doubt in her mind about that—but she had absolutely no idea what the play actually *was*.

I should have spent more time learning chess.

"So is this bad?" Coach Rex asked hesitantly.

THIS GUY. WHAT AN IDIOT.

Hush!

"Yeah," Destinee said. "It's bad."

Rex nodded slowly like he understood, then said, "So it's bad because …"

Destinee sighed. "God only knows." Then it seemed to occur to her what she'd said and she turned to Jessica. "*Does* He know?"

Do you know why this is bad?

OF COURSE.

Why is it bad?

BECAUSE JIMMY IS THE WORST.

Could you be more specific?

DO YOU WANT ME TO SPOIL THE ENDING FOR YOU?

She thought about the last divine spoiler he'd given her, how it'd left her stomach churning and her heart racing for the duration of the state championship, how she'd developed severe acid reflux in the days following the victory—though perhaps that was more from the fallout of kicking a hundred-yard field goal and kissing two different boys in the course of one evening on what turned out to be a national stage than it was from God's spoiler.

Six in one hand, half a dozen in the other, really.

No. Please don't.

She returned her attention to her mother, who was

waiting patiently. Rex seemed concerned. He was still having difficulty adjusting to Jessica's regular mental lapses while she spoke to her Father. "He said it's bad because Jimmy is the worst."

"Amen," Destinee said. "At least He's got that right."

REMIND HER OF THE MANY THINGS I GOT RIGHT THE NIGHT WE MET.

Nope. Go away.

TELL HER.

Isn't one of your commandments about jealousy?

COVETING. AND SHE'S NOT HIS WIFE, THANK ME. BESIDES, THAT DOESN'T APPLY TO ME BECAUSE I AM GOD.

So you keep saying.

SO YOU KEEP FORGETTING.

I wish.

Jessica headed back into the bathroom to finish her hair and put on a touch of mascara before she left for the night. There were a million ways Jimmy could use politics against her (and she had no doubt that was part of whatever dangerous web he was spinning), so there really wasn't a point in worrying about it yet, especially when she had more immediate things occupying her mind ...

To say she was nervous about attending her first kegger would be a gross understatement akin to saying Jesus had an okay pain tolerance or Moses had a poor sense of direction. Junior year had been such a whirlwind of football, media (mis)management, AP classes, and, whenever she had time, trying to maintain relationships, that parties never quite made it onto her radar. The busyness had served her well, though, when it came to avoiding drama. Sandra and Courtney and even Greg had tried to start it multiple times, prodding her with rumors and admittedly creative accusations to get a response, but she'd been too preoccupied to ever address the nonsense, so nothing had stuck. Finally her antagonizers gave up on using her as a source of sadistic entertainment and simply began ignoring her, which Jessica much preferred.

A knock on the front door pulled her from her anxious preening, and she heard her mother casually greeting Chris.

Best not to leave him alone with Destinee and Rex too long, though, so she hurriedly brushed her teeth, grabbed her shoes, and ran out into the living room to meet him.

"Hey." He looked her up and down and grinned. "You look ... pretty."

Pretty? She wanted to look hot. But maybe that's what he meant.

"Now remember," Destinee said in a lecturing tone that sounded one hundred percent synthetic, "no drunk driving."

Rex added, "Or tipsy driving."

Destinee's head hitched slightly to the side. "Well ... Yeah, probably that too. But you don't want to be a square at the party."

"Pretty sure God's got me covered," Jess said, itching to get out the door so she could, firstly, not have to worry about something embarrassing that would come out of her mother's mouth, and secondly, make out with Chris, who she hadn't seen in a good twenty-four hours since school let out for summer the day before.

"Be that as it may," Destinee said, "you can still get in a heap of trouble getting caught, even if you don't hurt nobody."

"I understand," Chris said. "You don't have to worry about it."

Destinee nodded, pacified, and Jess took that as her opportunity to herd Chris out the door.

"Oh wait!" said Destinee before they could even take two steps. "Wait here." She hurried into the kitchen and then came back out with a twelve-pack of Dos Equis cans. "You don't want to be the asswipes who show up without anything."

Jess shut her eyes. This was that embarrassing thing she'd tried to avoid; she just hadn't known it would take this form. She sighed and looked at Chris. He didn't seem embarrassed at all. "Thanks, Mrs. McCloud!" He stepped up and grabbed the case from her, grinning widely.

"Uh," spoke Rex from the couch, "I hate to be the one to say this ..."

Destinee turned toward him. "Then don't."

"But the football team has a strict no-alcohol policy."

She threw her fists onto her hips. "Is it football season?"

"Uh, no. But I mean ..."

She waved him off and then turned back to Jessica and Chris. "Go have fun. Tell Colton I said congrats, too."

"Will do," Chris said, but Jessica knew it probably wouldn't happen. From what she'd heard of Colton's graduation party, everyone from Mooremont and their cousins would be there. Chris and Jessica would be lucky if they even got a word in with Colton the whole night.

Chris opened the door and headed out toward his truck, and Jess paused when Destinee whispered her name. She turned back to look at her mother, wondering what it could be now.

"You got your …" Destinee made a ring with the thumb and pointer finger of her right hand and then poked the pointer finger of her left hand through it.

It took a second, but once she realized that her mother was pantomiming rolling a condom on a penis, her eyes darted over to Coach Rex. He squinted, still puzzling over the gesture. Jess shot her mom a harsh look and waved for her to put her hands down. "Yes. You put them in my purse this morning."

Destinee nodded. "Oh, that's right. Almost forgot."

Jess hadn't forgotten. Not that she would need condoms with Chris. Not yet, at least. Though she didn't know how much longer the center would hold on that.

She'd hardly set her purse down on the floorboards before Chris grabbed her and pulled her in for a kiss. After almost a year and a half, simply making out with him was still good enough for her. She was about seventy percent sure it was still good enough for him, too.

When he finally disengaged, he breathed in deeply and said, "I've missed you. I almost wish we didn't have to go to this party so I could have you all to myself."

Jess laughed. "We better get going. Miranda's gonna be pissed if we pick her up late again."

Chris frowned slightly, his brows pinching together as he shook his head. "No, we're not picking her up."

"I thought we were."

"No. I texted her to ask, but she already has a ride. Figured you knew."

"With who?"

"Quentin."

"Quentin Jones."

"Yep."

Jessica leaned back in her seat, staring vaguely ahead. "Huh."

"That's what I said, too."

So maybe she hadn't kept up with Miranda the past few weeks like she should have. She'd have to ask her once they arrived at the party. And speaking of which …

"You ever been to one of Colton's famous bonfires?" she asked.

Chris shook his head. "Nope."

"I don't know why," she said hesitantly, "but I'm kind of nervous."

She'd expected his reply to be the usual confident chuckle, followed by an assurance that he wouldn't let anything happen. But instead what he said was, "Yeah, me too."

Chapter Two

The F-350 crunched the gravel beneath its tires as it prowled down the Brookses' private drive. The ranch house came into view, backlit by the legendary bonfire that had been the setting for some of Mooremont's best rumors and gossip. Jess had never seen it herself, but if the intensity of the glow was any indication, it was just as large as everyone described it.

The truck turned sharply to the side and jolted to a skidding stop as Chris sucked in air. Jess jerked her head forward just in time to see the reason for the sudden veering.

"Oh shit. Is that Stephanie Lee?" Chris said a moment after the girl stumbled out of the path of the headlights that cut through the dust swirling in the still night air.

Jess squinted to get a better look. "A drunk version of her, at least."

"I almost killed her."

"Glad you didn't." Despite Stephanie preferring the

company of Sandra, Emma, and Courtney, she herself wasn't all that bad. Sure, she would smirk along with Courtney's frequent disses and giggle when Sandra hissed mean things about Jessica into her ear. But it still wasn't enough to leave Jess wishing Chris would take the girl out with his death machine of a truck. Plus, running over the only Asian student at Mooremont would most definitely be suspect, regardless of the circumstances. The last thing Jessica needed in her life right now was the judicial system.

As they pulled around the circular drive toward where the rest of the trucks and a Prius were parked, Jess got her first actual glimpse of the raging bonfire where dozens of silhouettes she couldn't identify wandered back and forth in what appeared to be an entirely aimless pattern.

"This is like ... a lot of people," she said hesitantly. Her aversion to crowds had only intensified in the past year as the news coverage of her life increased and people at Mooremont became more polarized as to whether she was the embodiment of good or evil. She longed for the days when most people were still on the fence about it.

"You'll be fine," Chris said. The confidence was back, but his words still lacked the necessary gusto to make them entirely believable.

He turned off the engine and climbed out, circling around to her side to open her door and help her down. Weaving her fingers with his, she followed a step behind him but only made it a few feet before she heard someone holler her name.

"Is that McCloud? And goddamn if that ain't Riley, too!" Colton shoved a girl that Jess didn't know off his lap where he sat on the rear bumper of a truck, and jogged over to them.

Chris held out the twelve-pack of Dos Equis. "We brought something. Happy graduation from Destinee McCloud."

Colton gasped and covered his heart with both hands. "It's exactly what I wanted!" He looked at Jess. "Your mom's still single, right?"

Jessica rolled her eyes. "You'll have to fight Coach Rex for her."

He inhaled like he was actually considering it. "Worth it."

"Don't think *she'll* mind?" Chris said, motioning at the girl who stood by the truck, waiting impatiently to pick up where she and Colton had left off.

He turned to see who Chris was referring to, then waved her off. "Psh. Nah. I can't shake that one, to be honest."

"She from Mooremont?" Jess asked.

"Mooremont? No. Elbow."

"Elbow?" Chris said hesitantly. "You sure you want to mess around with an Elbow girl? You know they have a reputation."

"Hey," Colton cut in quickly. "Easy with the slut shaming. That's my cousin you're talking about."

"Your cousin?" Jess said, hoping she'd misheard.

Colton shrugged. "Well, second cousin, I think. Listen, I'm probably not gonna bang her." He took the beer from Chris's arms and motioned for them to follow. "Keg's inside."

Not only was the keg inside, but so were probably seventy people, only some of whom Jess recognized from Mooretown. She kept her head down as she followed Chris who followed Colton, snaking through the musty crowd, and hoped that no one would notice her, thereby minimizing the odds for conflict. Why had she even bothered to come? What made her think a party with everyone she knew could be anything other than a bad idea? Maybe even the worst idea?

They'd just made it into the kitchen when a familiar face caught her attention.

"Miranda!"

Her best friend braced a hip against the counter as she faced Quentin, who was less than a foot away, his back to Jessica. He was leaning forward, his gaze aimed down toward Miranda who was tall for a girl, but still not close to Quentin's height. Jessica immediately recognized his posture as one she'd seen from Miranda's current perspective many times during her fake relationship with him.

"Miranda!" Jess called again, and that seemed to snap her out of her trance. She looked over at Jessica and her face lit up.

"Jess! I wondered when you were coming!" She hustled over and gave her a hug, but before Jess released her, she whispered into Miranda's ear, "Why didn't you tell me about Quentin?"

Miranda chuckled and pulled away, back to her new fling. "It's recent, don't worry. We started talking at the athletic banquet on Tuesday."

Jess nodded and grinned. "Okay then."

"He's leaving for UT in a few months, so it's nothing serious," Miranda added.

Jess held up her hands in mock surrender. "Hey, I'm not judging. He was a fun fake boyfriend."

Even just seeing Miranda—and Quentin, too, actually—helped to calm Jess's nerves.

"Here." She turned at the sound of Chris's voice behind her to find him extending a Solo cup of beer her way. What kind of beer? Probably didn't matter.

She drank it as quickly as she could.

Quentin sauntered over. "Jessica McCloud! My favorite child of God!" He grabbed her and pulled her in for a hug, planting a sloppy kiss on her cheek. He pulled back slightly and mumbled, "He doesn't mind if I say that, right?" His eyes flickered up toward the ceiling.

"No, I think it's fine."

Quentin nodded and stepped back, and Jessica glanced over at Chris. When she saw that he was laughing at Quentin's display, she was able to relax a little herself.

"This joker still treating you right?" Quentin asked, nodding at Chris.

Chris threw him a middle finger.

Jess grinned as she felt the first effects of the beer start to relax the muscles around her lips. "Yeah, he's all right, I guess."

Quentin pointed at Chris. "Better stay that way. If I have to drive my black ass back from Austin to this shitty, racist town to beat your ass, Riley, I'm gonna make it count."

Chris chuckled. "Easy there. And don't you think that

her Father probably has the ass beating covered if I fuck up?"

Clearly Quentin had never thought of that, and he nodded and ahh-ed as the idea sank in.

"Also," Jessica added, trying not to let her annoyance spoil her mood, "don't forget that I can handle my own life."

"Oh yeah!" Quentin shouted excitedly. "I forgot you can smite! Ha! Riley, you better not try nothing, or she'll smite that big ol' dick of yours right off!"

Miranda spat out a small portion of her mouthful of beer before swallowing down the rest then allowing herself to howl with laughter. Chris chuckled along uncomfortably, and Jess realized that this was *not* the first time such an idea had occurred to him.

Huh. Maybe that's why he's never tried anything.

Most of Jessica's teammates had graduated that morning, so she made the rounds, tracking them down, saying bye for now, apologizing for missing graduation. It was a deliberate move, though, and most of them seemed to not only understand, but also appreciate the gesture, which had allowed them to have their time in the spotlight.

The night flew by, and hours later Jessica found herself fully content and relaxed, leaning back in a lawn chair by the bonfire, Chris to her left, Stephanie Lee chugging a glass of water someone had mercifully brought her to Jessica's right.

She turned when she heard Eddie's voice hollering from the house behind them. "Riley! Where's that beer you brought?"

Chris turned in his chair as Eddie approached. "It should be in the fridge. That's where Colton put it."

Eddie pressed his lips together in a frown. "Fridge is empty."

"Well fuck. That's what the keg's for."

"Keg's floated."

"Oh."

Stephanie's speech was severely impaired as she hollered, "We're outta beer?"

"Easy, girl," Eddie said curtly. "You don't get anything else tonight anyway." He turned back toward Chris. "Yeah, guess we're outta booze."

"Don't Colton's parents have a liquor cabinet?" Marcus Mason asked, his massive frame appearing from the other side of the fire. His hands rested on his hips, and he looked more serious than Jess had ever seen him, even during the past two championship games.

"They do," Eddie said, "but it's locked up."

More people had gathered around at the signs of controversy and began asking the same questions over and over again. "Wait, we're outta booze?" Drew Fenster said.

Eddie nodded concernedly.

Dennis Rivera, arms folded across his chest, appeared behind Eddie. "Wait, there's no more booze?"

Eddie nodded again.

Gary Higgins, Jess's once temporary biology partner and well-known busty cat lady enthusiast appeared next to the fire on the other side of Stephanie. *Who the hell invited Gary?* "You mean there's no beer left?"

"God dammit, Gary," Jess said, irritated by his presence.

"Yes. He's just said it three times." She looked to Chris. "I guess it's late anyway. We should probably head out."

The voice of a person she'd done a good job of avoiding all night cut through the worried murmurs of the group that had amassed around Eddie, Chris, and herself. "Hey Jessica. If you're really the daughter of God, why don't you just turn some water into wine for us?"

Trent Wurst shoved his way past Gary and grabbed Stephanie's glass of water, holding it out toward Jessica. "Come on, Girl Christ. Can you perform miracles or not?"

"God dammit, Trent," Chris spat, standing from his chair. "You should know better." His former friend stared at him, and a meaningful look passed between the two boys that left Jess wondering if Trent might actually back down. But then he scoffed. "What, Chris, worried you might be banging the Antichrist?"

The group around them had gone silent. Jess stayed silent, too, wondering what Chris might say as a response. Would he say they still hadn't had sex? Or would he lie and say they had?

But instead he took a drastically different approach. "That's not a nice thing to call your mom."

The crowd responded accordingly with "ooooh"s and cackles.

Trent's lips curled into a snarl. "Good one, Chris. But my mom's not a slut like yours and Jessica's. Doesn't matter. Obviously she can't do a simple thing like turn water into wine, but I coulda told you that. Because she's not God's daughter." Trent seemed pleased with himself and swigged from the bottle of Big Red he clutched in his fist. The coloring had dyed the skin just above his lips in a small semicircle that overlapped onto his blond, wispy attempt at a mustache.

There was nothing that Jessica wanted to do more in that moment than turn that *fucking* water into *fucking* wine. Except maybe turn Big Red into cyanide.

PROBABLY DON'T WANT TO TRY IT.

Why not?

BECAUSE IT'S NOT ONE OF YOUR MIRACLES.

Oh, now you're all about telling me what my miracles are?

ONLY BECAUSE I HATE THIS KID.

Can I smite him?

NOPE.

She remembered a phrase she'd heard Mrs. Thomas use when the woman had added custom-made football pads that fit Jessica's feminine frame to the school athletic budget: *Better to beg for forgiveness than ask for permission.*

Yep. That sounded good.

The glass of water exploded in Trent's hand, and the shock caused him to spill his Big Red down his front and arms. For a moment nobody moved, not even Trent. But as the Big Red started to mingle with the blood from his fingers, causing the whole scene to seem much gorier than it actually was, Jessica knew two things. First, she'd established her place in the annals of Brooks bonfire lore, and secondly, it was time to head out. And quick.

Chris didn't need telling. As soon as she was out of her seat, he was behind her, his hand on her lower back, pushing her toward the ranch house. Courtney Wurst flew by them at the sound of her brother's screams, and Jess put a little extra hop in her step to avoid having to face the wrath of the Wurst sister once she pieced together what had happened. They were almost all the way through the house and out the front door when Jess remembered. "Miranda. We should grab her. Quentin is way too drunk to drive."

Chris nodded. "Okay. Then we should grab Quentin, too."

"Are *you* good to drive?"

He nodded. "Yeah, I stopped drinking like an hour ago. I'm fine."

Neither Miranda nor Quentin had been out by the bonfire, so Jess took the house while Chris headed out front to search.

Living room? She took a few steps in, peeked around. Nope. A couple writhed together on the couch, and a few more looked only minutes away from taking things outside to writhe in the back of a truck, but no Miranda or Quentin.

She checked the kitchen again but quickly ducked out when she sensed the restlessness of people as the news of no more booze spread from person to person, sometimes needing to be repeated multiple times before it penetrated the drunkenness.

She headed down the hallway toward rows of doors, stopping at the bathroom. Someone was in there, judging by the light coming out from under it and the sound of retching.

She knocked. "Miranda?"

When a male voice responded, she asked, "Quentin?"

"No! Leave me alone! I'm fine."

Not Quentin. Maybe there was another bathroom somewhere.

She wandered down the hall and poked her head into another room.

"Oh shit."

The light was off, but enough illumination from the bonfire made its way through the open blinds for Jess to make out two figures on the bed in varying degrees of undress. "Miranda! God dammit, Miranda ..."

Her friend looked up from where she was pinned underneath Quentin. "Jessica!"

Finally Quentin seemed to notice that they weren't alone, and his eyes shot open and he leapt off the bed, his arms raised above his head. "She told me to!"

As he stood there in only his boxer briefs, Jessica tried not to stare. She turned her gaze to Miranda instead. "Oh sheesh. Put on your shirt. And pants. It's time to go."

Quentin hopped back into his clothing quickly, but it took a little searching before Miranda was able to locate her shorts and tank top to slip on again.

Jessica waited impatiently outside the bedroom door until they emerged again. "Party's over. Time to get the hell out."

A shrill female voice hollered from the back door in the kitchen, "McCloud!"

"Shit."

Miranda's head jerked in the general direction of the sound. "Wait, what happened? Who's yelling for you?"

"Sounds like Courtney. We gotta go. I'll explain in the truck."

Quentin and Miranda were compliant from there on out as they followed Jess to the front door, where Chris was just about to walk through. "Found 'em," Jessica said.

"Where were they?"

"Tell you later. Let's get out of here. Courtney's pissed."

That was all she had to say until they were loaded up into the truck—Jessica in the front, Quentin and Miranda in the back seat, already putting hands on each other.

As Chris steered the truck in the necessary zigzags to avoid the potholes in the gravel, Jess glanced in the back seat to see Miranda and Quentin trying to steady themselves on each other as they continued a sloppy attempt at sucking face.

The truck's front tire was jolted by a sneaky pothole and the driver's side of the truck bobbed up and down, sending Miranda's forehead into Quentin's nose. They both groaned at the pain, and Jess turned away to face front. Maybe that'd cause them to cool it. There was something terribly disconcerting about seeing her best friend like this.

"I think we should probably drop off Quentin first," Jessica suggested. A tough-love conversation with Miranda seemed in order before they could leave her at her mom's house. Cheyenne Forte wouldn't be thrilled about Miranda's state, so the girl needed to pull it together, hurry to bed, and sleep it off before her mother caught on.

"That works," Chris said, squinting through the high beams at the dusty road ahead. "Quentin! Where do you live?"

"Palo Alto Road." With his hands still cupped around his nose, the words came out muffled and Chris made him repeat it louder.

"I'm only about half sure I know where that is," he mumbled so only Jess could hear.

"Are you sure you're good to drive?" she asked. The amount of concentration he seemed to be exerting just to keep the truck on the road hinted that he was *not* good to drive.

"Yeah, I told you, I stopped drinking an hour ago."

"You seem anxious, I guess."

"I am anxious!"

Taken aback by his tone, she decided it was best to not reply, and finally they made it onto a paved farm-to-market road.

Chris's anxiety didn't dissipate, though. In fact, it only intensified. When she glanced at him again, there was a vein bulging in his neck and another bulging in his temple. Was it the exploding glass? Was that what had him so anxious?

Sure, there was a good chance he had a little PTSD from kindergarten, but who didn't?

Still, though, it was like his heart rate was emitting rapid pulses into the cab of the truck, making her heart race as well. As the truck slowed down for a four-way stop, Jessica looked into the back seat again. Apparently Quentin's nose felt much better now.

"For God's sake," she said, "at least put on your seat belts."

Then she immediately regretted the order, as Quentin

unlocked his lips from Miranda's, buckled himself in, and then used buckling Miranda as an excuse to wrap his arms around her and grab a fistful of her ass while he leaned over.

Rolling her eyes, Jessica turned to face front again. What was her duty as best friend here? Should she try to stop Miranda, who was obviously too intoxicated to make any important decisions, or should she let her continue? She seemed to be enjoying Quentin's hands on her. And they'd arrived at the party together, so perhaps she'd been hoping for this the whole time, even before she got trashed.

Jess continued philosophizing over her social obligation as the F-350 pulled past the stop sign.

For a truck as large as Chris's, the thing had giddy-up and go, and as he accelerated into the intersection, a sedan, headlights off, blew through the stop sign on their left. Jessica's mind hardly had time to sync with her peripheral vision before the moment of impact.

The car clipped the front of the truck and jolted them, locking Jess's seatbelt to hold her in place as the truck spun clockwise. Less than a second had passed and the sequence of events already began to tangle together in her mind—had she seen the car first or heard Chris hiss, "Shit!" first?

The sedan spun in a tight circle until centrifugal force sent it rolling on its side—once, twice, five times—until it came to rest, nose down in a trench on the side of the road.

"Oh my god! What just happened?" Miranda slurred from the back seat.

Jessica was too stunned to reply. She did a quick mental

It's a Miracle!

sweep of her body, found she was okay, and glanced over at Chris, whose side of the vehicle had taken the brunt of the collision.

"Are you okay?" she croaked above the sound of deflating airbags.

His eyes were opened so wide that the lids were completely invisible. His jaw hung slightly open as he continued to white-knuckle the steering wheel.

Quentin moaned in the back seat, and it seemed to break whatever spell of horror Chris was under.

"Shit," Chris said. "Fuckin' *shit*."

"Are you okay?" Jess asked more urgently. Chris nodded quickly.

It wasn't until she'd hopped out of the truck that Jessica could fully assess the damage, which was thankfully minimal. The driver's side headlight had been completely demolished, but the rest of the truck was mostly unharmed, and his deer guard was scratched, but otherwise fine. The one headlight that remained was pointed ten yards to the left of where the sedan had finally come to a rest, allowing only the softest, outermost light of the beam to land upon the wreckage. As she and Chris jogged up to the car, smoke poured out of hood, and a change in wind direction sent it blowing into Jessica's mouth and nose. She coughed and waved at the air in front of her face, trying to clear it.

The wind changed again as Jessica made it to edge of the road. And it was just before she'd started down the incline toward the driver's window, which she could tell even from this distance had shattered and fallen out, that she noticed the bumper sticker.

"Oh shit."

Chris paused before he headed down. "What? What is it?"

She grabbed his arm and pulled him next to her, directing his attention at the sticker, which might as well have read, *Congrats, Jessica! You're officially fucked!*

"We're fucked," Chris said, and Jessica's eyes lingered on the bumper sticker for a moment longer, hoping maybe the words would magically change to something other than they were:

White Light Church
Sumus omnes porcos, sed Deus est Aper.

Chapter Three

If someone had presented the current situation to Jessica as a hypothetical—"Imagine you're heading back from a party with your boyfriend where you've both been drinking underage, and he T-bones a car in the middle of the night, causing that car to roll multiple times before landing in a ditch on the side of the road, smoke bellowing from the hood …"—and then asked her "How could this be worse?" she would likely have said, "I don't know, make it a member of White Light Church."

They were a scourge upon her life.

But that didn't mean she wanted to be partially responsible for the death of any of the members. Or at least, she didn't want to get in legal trouble on account of it.

"Shit," Chris said for the umpteenth time since the collision. "Shit, shit, shit."

Jess didn't disagree.

There was nothing that could be done for it, though, and that smoke sure was issuing wildly from the hood, so the next logical step was to pull whoever was *inside* the car *out* of the car and to safety. Even that plan, though, had one major flaw.

There was no one inside the car. Jessica discovered it as soon as she'd made her way down the slope, rolling her ankle slightly on an unseen rock, to stand by the driver's side door. Not a single person.

Is this a ghost car? She'd heard of ghost ships, but she wasn't sure exactly how she felt about ghosts in general. Did they exist? How had she never spoken with her Father about this? She needed to start a list of things to ask Him about and have it on hand all the time for when He decided to show up. Then she could simply go down item by item, mining for answers. Item number one would be, *Ghosts— What about them?*

But she knew she wouldn't remember to make such a list.

The question of ghosts and their means of transportation flew completely out the window when she realized that whoever was driving this car had flown out the window as well. The hole in the windshield was just the right size for someone to have been ejected headfirst through it. That made more sense, though it wasn't any more comforting than the idea of a ghost car. At least no one could be killed in a ghost car.

Chris appeared over her shoulder, blocking out what small bit of headlight illuminated the scene. "Driver flew out," she said.

"What do we do?" He sounded like he might hyperventilate. She turned toward him and put a hand on each of his shoulders. "We find the person who was in there. Maybe they need help." But looking at the level of damage and the fact that she couldn't hear any movement among the brush, it was more likely the need would be for a large black bag.

"My football career is over before it began," he said airily, looking like he'd just woken up from a long, vivid dream and was trying to piece it together in his mind.

"It's fine. We'll figure this out." Why did she have to be the sane one?

And where in the hell was God?

Why have you forsaken me?

She'd had that thought before, but it'd always felt a bit heavy handed and melodramatic. Until now. It seemed appropriate now.

The truck doors slammed twice just as she was about to continue into the roadside brush to search for the driver. She turned back toward the F-350 and hollered, "Get back in the truck!"

Her tone must have accurately conveyed the direness of the situation because Quentin and Miranda didn't take another step forward before they returned to the back seat.

Jess scanned the scrub brush. A National Geographic on nocturnal animals surfaced in her mind. Humans weren't currently nocturnal, but the presence of so many rods in the human eye indicated that they once were. She wished (not for the first time, oddly) that she could have margay eyes with their acute night vision, but she settled for using the trick she'd learned from that particular episode and focused her attention on her peripheral vision, hoping it would allow her to catch some sign of movement that her eyes' cones would miss.

Nothing.

The driver could have been ejected at any point in the flip and in any direction, Jessica realized, so she might as well get started searching. But somehow it only took a dozen intuitive steps before she found the driver, who was facedown, one arm stretched out to the side, the other bent at a horrifying angle and draped over the back of the person's head.

"Shit, it's a woman," Chris said, and Jess wasn't sure why that mattered.

"Or a man in a dress," she said.

"Huh?"

She grimaced and waved him off. "I don't know. I'm just saying."

"Hey you!" Chris shouted at the woman or man in a dress. "You dead?"

Jess smacked his arm and hissed, "You don't ask someone if they're dead."

"What?"

"It's ... impolite."

Chris nodded as if he understood and recovered with, "I mean, you alive?"

There was still no response.

"Maybe she's just unconscious," Jessica suggested as she took another hesitant step forward.

"Or he," Chris corrected, keeping his distance.

"Right."

Jessica kneeled next to the body then, with pincher fingers, grabbed the wrist of the twisted arm and removed it from the back of the head, placing it in a position that almost looked the way an arm might lie if someone had simply fallen asleep on their stomach. Then she rolled the body onto its side to get a better look and see if she could detect signs of life.

The blood covering the woman's face seeping from the row of lacerations along her forehead almost prevented Jessica from recognizing who it was. But then suddenly it clicked into place.

It was no man in a dress.

It was Mrs. Wurst.

She dropped the body, and it rolled back onto its face. "Shitballs." She jumped up.

"Was that ..." Chris whispered. She glanced back at him, and he was hugging himself tightly and covering his mouth like he might puke.

"We killed Mrs. Wurst," she said. "We killed Mrs. Wurst."

"No! Take her pulse! Maybe she's alive!"

There was nothing Jessica wanted to do less at that moment than touch the presumed corpse of this woman who had, yet again, proven herself to be a thorn in Jessica's crown.

But she needed to be sure. So she reached down and placed two fingers on the woman's neck, like she'd been taught to do for her CPR certification in health class the previous year.

Where was the pulse? Maybe she got the wrong spot.

She tried another place, closer to the jawline. "Am I ... do I have the right place?"

"Maybe more to the side," Chris coached, but clearly he had less of an idea than she did.

"Nothing," she said, leaning back onto her heels.

"Check for breathing," Chris suggested.

"How do I do that?"

"Hold a mirror right in front of her mouth."

"A *mirror?*"

He nodded adamantly. "Yeah, like a hand mirror."

So Chris was no help. "Do you have a goddamn hand mirror?!"

"No. I'm sorry! I don't know what to do!"

The blood was starting to dry on Mrs. Wurst's face, and Jessica's mind raced through scenarios where she and Chris could get off scot-free for this.

Maybe Mrs. Wurst was just on her way home from strangling babies.

Or maybe Mrs. Wurst was in a lot of pain and we simply dealt her a merciful death.

No, neither of those would exonerate them. They were screwed.

Chris ran his fingers compulsively through his hair as he began pacing back and forth. "My career is over ..."

"It wasn't your fault. She ran the stop sign."

"That doesn't matter. I've been drinking."

Jessica didn't take her eyes off Mrs. Wurst. Maybe there was a sign of life she was missing. "Should we call the cops?"

"Oh," Chris yelled, melodramatically, "you mean her

husband? Yeah, he's gonna *love* this. We're so screwed, Jess. He's gonna put our heads on stakes."

She wished he'd shut up for just a second.

CPR. She'd have to try it. It was the last resort.

She rolled Ruth Wurst over onto her back, cringing at the crunching of bones in the misshapen arm as the weight of her body rolled over it.

How did CPR work again? Chest compressions, right.

She steadied herself, rested one hand over the other, and then lowered them down toward Mrs. Wurst's heart, thinking, *Please let this work*, over and over again.

And the moment her palm made contact with Mrs. Wurst's chest, Jessica felt a familiar force move through her, one that she'd come to associate with football and smiting. It was like a weak magnet pulsed through her torso, down her arms, and the pull of it moved out through her sweaty palms, tugging lose.

And then suddenly the dead body in front of her lurched and began gasping for air. Jessica yanked her hands away to hover over Mrs. Wurst without touching her.

What in God's name ...

IT'S A MIRACLE.

No. Please no.

ISN'T THIS WHAT YOU WANTED?

I mean, partly yes, partly no.

YEAH, I GET THAT.

Mrs. Wurst's eyes shot open and found Jessica's face immediately.

Only just managing to regain control of her bladder before an already terrible situation was made even worse,

Jessica froze in place, unsure what her next move should be.

But luckily she was spared the decision, because just as Ruth murmured, "Jessica?" she felt Chris's hands slip underneath her armpits and lift her back up onto her feet.

"We gotta get the hell out of here," he said, and Jess was inclined to agree. She scrambled after Chris up the incline, back onto the road, and toward the remaining headlight, not looking back once, not even when Ruth Wurst's voice hollered her name a second, third, and forth time.

As she jumped back into the cab, Quentin began demanding answers. "Call 9-1-1," was all she said to him. "Report a rollover accident and then hang up. Don't give them your name. And try to sound less drunk."

Quentin nodded and did as he was told.

"Fuck," Chris said, straining to turn the steering wheel. "Power steering is out."

"Then use those goddamn muscles, Chris," Jessica yelled, "and get us the hell out of here."

She tried to avoid looking at the wreckage of the Wurst car on the side of the road as they pulled away. Even as they began to put distance between themselves and the wreck, the acrid smell of burnt rubber and the suffocating mugginess of exhaust seemed ever present, clouding her panicked thoughts until two truths finally broke through the fog and left her no less frantic than before. Firstly, she had finally discovered another miracle, but seeming more pertinent: she'd just been a part of a deadly hit and run.

After a moment's consideration of her life so far, she

decided that these two things being linked was about par for the course.

*   *   *

She knew she shouldn't have this raw craving, considering the events of the night so far, but as Chris's truck idled in the McCloud driveway, Jessica needed nothing more than to feel his hands on her. She pulled him close and he seemed to want the same.

He did away with her shirt quickly, and as she looked down at herself, though she couldn't actually remember putting on a black bra (or even owning one), she was glad she had. Chris seemed happy with it, too, and he dove forward, their lips crashing only a moment before he grabbed a handful of her breast.

It was probably a strange time for her to lose her virginity, but it *felt* like a great time. The best time, even.

But as absorbed with Chris Riley as she was—the roughness of his fingertips, the softness of his lips, the woodsy smell of him—she also became aware that his broken headlight was now back on. That was good, she supposed. She tried to forget about it, but it nagged at her, and her mind kept returning to the solution it hinted at, even as Chris reached around her back and unclasped her sexy black bra in one deft snap of his fingers.

Then a figure passed in front of the beam of the magically repaired headlight, then across the beam of the light on the passenger's side, and she immediately recognized that the figure and the repaired headlight were related.

Well, since it was a dream, she might as well make the most of it.

A moment later, when she heard a tap at the window, she swatted Chris's hands away from her belt and then re-clasped her bra and slipped her shirt back on before rolling down the window to say hello to her half-brother.

"What do you want?"

"Is that any way to talk to family?"

She heard Chris mumble a confused, "Jesus?" and she nodded but otherwise ignored him.

"I found another miracle. La-di-da."

Jesus narrowed his eyes at her. "I sense you're being disingenuous with your enthusiasm."

"Yep."

"Well, you should be happy."

"And why's that? We're now wanted in a hit and run."

He blew a short raspberry and waved off her concern. "Minor details. God's plan has you covered, I'm sure."

She arched an eyebrow at him. "Really? You're sure about that?"

He paused with his mouth open for a second, one eye twitched, and then his confidence returned. "Yes. Besides, raising people from the dead was one of my favorite miracles."

"Wait, you could do it, too?"

Jesus sighed impatiently. "You know, I'm pretty sure I've mentioned this to you before."

"Then clearly I wasn't paying attention. Maybe someday we could have a conversation when I'm not horny and preoccupied and then I'd listen to you."

Jesus shut his eyes and pinched the bridge of his nose. "The point," he said once he finally looked up again, "is that resurrecting people is a good miracle to have."

"I'd argue it depends on who you resurrect."

He seemed to consider it. "Okay, I can see where you're coming from."

"Did you ever resurrect any real asswipes?"

"*Oh* yeah. I just kept those off the record. I actually tried to keep them all off the record, but John pulled a fast one with Lazarus long after I was dead, and it'd already been published before I could pay him a little visit."

Jessica struggled to follow along; what she really wanted was to forget this whole conversation and go back to the part where Chris undid her bra. "Wait. Who is Lazarus?"

"You— How have you not heard of Lazarus?"

"Is that a Bible thing?"

Jesus appraised her dubiously. "Yeah, it's a Bible thing."

"See? There it is. I've never read the Bible. Dad told me to wait for the second edition. There's stuff He needs to fix first."

Jesus stroked his beard. "I see. What sort of stuff will He change?"

"Mostly stuff about menstruation, I think."

The mention of it caused Jesus to gasp and then choke slightly. He pounded at his chest until he was able to regain his composure.

Jessica rolled her eyes. "Don't tell me you're uncomfortable with it, too."

Jesus angled his head toward her meaningfully. "Well, it *is* unclean."

"No, not anymore. God changed that."

"He what?"

"He changed that. It's clean now. Well, I mean, it's still messy, but it's not *un*clean."

Jesus shut his eyes tightly to reset. "Sheesh, I keep telling Him to keep me updated when He changes His mind, but you know how He can be."

She knew. "Terrible communicator. Doesn't work well on a team."

"Exactly!" Jesus yelled excitedly. "Oh mankind, it's so nice having someone else who gets it."

From behind her, Chris blurted, "Thank you."

She turned to him. "Huh? For what?"

But Chris was looking past her. "Not you, Him. Thank you for dying for our sins."

"You're welcome," Jesus said humbly.

Jessica turned back toward her half-brother. "Why are you here anyway?"

"Oh, just wanted to say good luck. Like I said, raising the dead was my favorite miracle, but you need to use discretion. I made the mistake of being a bit showy with Lazarus, and it didn't work out well for me. Granted, it saved the souls of all mankind, but, well, you know. Those Romans had to go all out with the torture thing. A bunch of meanies when you get right down to it."

Jessica wasn't in the mood to think about her ultimate fate. All she really wanted was to get laid. "You're kind of a downer. Can you leave?"

"Yep." He poofed, vanishing into a cloud of white, semi-fluorescent smoke that swirled where he had once stood.

She turned back to Chris. "Where were we?"

But he no longer seemed in the mood.

Dammit! This is my *dream! Get in the mood!*

She tried to make it happen, but he wasn't complying. Instead, he said, "Do you hear that?"

She heard nothing. "Nope."

"Listen, it's like a jackhammer or something."

This was getting ridiculous. She pulled off her shirt to see if she could draw him in. But he simply closed his eyes. "No, I can still hear it. How do you not hear it?"

Well, it was her dream, so she could do what she wanted. "Shut up about it." She climbed on top of him, despite his distracted attempts to push her away. She straddled him in the tight space between the driver's seat and the steering wheel and leaned down to kiss him before he poofed right out of existence too. "What the hell?"

Worst sex dream ever.

Part of her expected the dream to end, for her to wake up, but it didn't. "What am I supposed to do now?" She started by putting her shirt back on, and then she waited patiently in the cab for the dream to disappear or for something to happen.

It felt like hours in her dream world before she awoke to the darkness of her room. There was a knock on her window and she sat up in bed and looked over to find Chris's face pressed up against the glass.

He looked panicked. Well, no surprise there.

She crawled out from under the sheets and slid open her window. "What's up?"

"I can't sleep. I'm so screwed, Jess." He sounded like he was going to cry. She hoped to her Father he wouldn't cry in front of her.

"Just ... Here," she said. "Go to the front door. You can come in."

He shook his head adamantly. "I don't want to piss off your mom."

Part of Jessica's mind was still stuck in the cab of Chris's dream truck, and she struggled to focus her attention on the task at hand. "Please, she'd be proud if I snuck you in. Meet you at the front door."

By the time she was able to slip on a bra under the loose T-shirt she'd worn to bed and amble to the front door, Chris was already there, waiting, bouncing anxiously on his toes. She could tell that his hands, which were shoved into his shorts pockets, were balled into nervous fists.

Maybe she should be as anxious as he was, but she was too tired. Sleep hadn't come easily. In the hour between when she'd laid down in bed and actually fallen asleep, her thoughts had become a hellish smoothie with a base of adrenaline, one part Chris's future, two parts her own future, and seventeen parts mental images of Mrs. Wurst's mangled body and the look in her eyes when they finally opened and stared up at Jessica.

"You want some water?" she asked, as he stepped inside.

"Water?" He seemed to have difficulty registering the word.

"Yeah. Are you thirsty?"

"Uh, I guess so."

She headed into the kitchen and he followed.

Once she'd convinced him to sit in a chair at the table, she passed him his glass, which he promptly ignored. "What are we gonna do?"

"We have a plan, Chris. We just need to stick to it." But as her mind became more alert, the doubt and panic crawled back in. "It's not like we killed anyone."

His jaw dropped and his head leaned toward her. "No, Jess, that's *exactly* what we did."

"Well, I mean, sure. But I brought her back."

Chris nearly jumped into the ceiling when the hall light flicked on behind him.

"Is that Chris I hear?" Destinee was up.

Chris's eyes opened wide, and he looked at Jessica for a cue. She shrugged slightly. "Yeah, Mom. It's Chris."

At least her mother had done them the favor of wrapping herself up modestly in a fuzzy robe before coming out to see what all the commotion was. Small victories.

Her mascara had smudged from sleep, creating dark circles beneath her squinty eyes as she entered into the kitchen and went straight to making herself a glass of ice water. She leaned against the counter and glanced at the clock, which Jess hadn't even thought of doing yet. "Already five thirty. Y'all just get home?"

Chris was smart enough to stay silent and let Jessica

take the lead with her mother. "No. I got home a while ago."

Destinee pressed her lips together and nodded, like she understood, but the creases that appeared on her forehead made it clear she did not. "So, y'all just been talking, or … ?" As she glanced from one face to the other, she started to clue in. "What happened?"

Jessica's gut told her to come clean. The situation was already messy enough, and lying would only make it more complicated, especially since Jess wasn't feeling particularly creative in her hazy mental state. Besides, Destinee would likely be happy to hear that Jessica had discovered another miracle.

So she decided to lead with that. "I discovered another miracle."

Destinee almost spit out the sip of water she'd just taken, but she managed to swallow it down quickly before croaking out, "No shit! How'd that happen?"

Jess made the mistake of glancing at Chris, whose clenched jaw indicated he clearly thought honesty was *not* going to be the best policy, but she continued anyway. Her mom wasn't exactly a law-abiding citizen and, given the circumstance, they could use another ally in this whole mess. "Well, so, we were leaving the party, and we came to this stop sign. Chris did everything right. He stopped, looked, then went forward. But another car didn't have its lights on and came barreling through and it clipped the front of Chris's truck—"

"Everyone all right?" Destinee interrupted.

"Ehh … more or less," Jessica hedged.

Destinee narrowed her eyes. "More or less?" she echoed suspiciously.

Jessica took a deep breath. Time to rip off the Band-Aid. "It was Mrs. Wurst. She died."

Destinee blinked quickly three times, but otherwise showed no signs of having heard. Then slowly. "I'm not sure how I feel about that."

"I brought her back to life, though," Jess added, realizing as she said it how little it actually helped the gravity of the situation.

Destinee blinked again. "I'm not sure how I feel about that, either." Then it apparently sank in, and her glazed over expression sharpened. "Wait. You brought her back from the dead? That's your miracle?"

Jessica nodded.

"Well hot damn, baby!" But while her voice sounded celebratory, her face was still squished up toward the center, her nose crinkled, eyebrows pinched together. "So then what happened?"

"Well …" Jess looked at Chris, and when she caught his eye, he chuckled. Then the chuckle turned into a cackle.

Okay, so Chris was going through some stuff.

Jess pushed forward. "We got in the truck and drove off."

Destinee slowly pulled her gaze from Chris's minor breakdown to refocus on her daughter. "That's a hit and run."

"Right."

"That's illegal."

"I know."

Still leaning against the counter, Destinee covered her mouth with her fingers and stared at the linoleum kitchen floor while she considered it. "But it was probably a good call."

"That's what we thought."

Destinee turned, grabbed the coffee pot and began filling it with tap water from the sink. "Well, this sure is something."

Chris's laughter subsided, but not before tears streamed down his face.

All in all, his had been a pretty seamless mental breakdown. Quick, harmless. And he had a good laugh. It couldn't have been that bad.

As the coffee began brewing, the familiar bubbling and bitter aroma filling the kitchen, Destinee took a seat at the table between Chris and Jessica. "What'd you do with the truck?"

"Hid it," Jessica said. "In a couple days Chris is going to report that he hit a deer."

"What kind of damage was there?"

Chris was the one to answer now. "Took out the front light, scratched up the deer guard, took out the power steering."

Destinee frowned and shook her head. "Deer couldn't have done that to *your* truck. Better say it was a hog."

It was no small comfort to Jess that her mother was now officially a co-conspirator.

"And you said she saw you before you ran off?"

Jessica nodded, and her mom had to think hard about

that. "Well, maybe she was fucked up and didn't recognize you."

"Maybe," Jess said hesitantly, "but she did call me by my name. Like a dozen times."

"Well, balls! Then I suspect the chief'll be after you." She glanced at the clock again. "How long ago was it?"

It felt like two weeks, but Jess knew that couldn't be right. Chris answered for her. "About four hours ago. Quentin called 9-1-1, so they should've found her by now."

"Quentin?" she asked, looking at Jessica. "Your ex?"

"Fake ex," Chris corrected. "And yeah. He and Miranda were in the back seat. She didn't see them, though, and they promised not to say anything."

Destinee looked doubtfully at her daughter. "Miranda promised … ?"

Jess nodded. "I know, I know. But there's nothing we can do about that. I know she'll *try* not to let it slip."

"I've no doubt about that," Destinee said. "Never seen someone try so hard to be a good friend. But, you know how she is." Destinee paused, narrowed her eyes at something on the wall opposite her, and rubbed her chin. "You know, if this happened four hours ago, and no one's come knocking on our front door looking for you, there's a chance that Ruth doesn't remember who it was."

"Or she re-died," Chris added, unhelpfully.

"*Or*," Jess said, glaring at him, "she remembered that we know about her affair with Jimmy."

It'd been the kernel of hope she'd latched onto during the long, silent ride between Miranda's house and her own.

She'd even asked God about it to make sure she had the fail-safe.

Are Mrs. Wurst and Jimmy still knocking boots?

OH YEAH. KNOCKING BOOTS, BUMPING UGLIES, FLOGGING ... WELL, JUST FLOGGING.

So maybe that was why the whole of the Mooretown police wasn't beating down her door.

But Destinee waved her off. "Nah, I think we've used that one up. We can't just keep knocking Ruth around and hoping she stays quiet because she don't want her husband to find out about her nasty-ass affair."

"Who's having a nasty-ass affair?" came another voice from the hallway.

This time Jessica almost jumped up to the ceiling before she laid eyes on Coach Rex.

He was fully clothed, like maybe they'd think he'd simply crashed on Destinee's bedroom floor, rather than the obvious reality. Jess struggled to hide her disgust.

"Ruth Wurst and Jimmy Dean," Destinee said casually.

"I could see it," he said before clearing gunk from his throat and heading directly to where the coffeemaker was finishing up. He grabbed four mugs from the cabinet and then filled them and served them black to everyone at the table, taking his own with him over to the empty seat.

"So here's the plan," Destinee said, "and you can fill Quentin and Miranda in on it. We're going to do nothing. You're going to lay low for a couple days, then Chris, you're going to report that you hit a hog. Then that's it. No one says a thing."

Coach Rex chuckled. "Goddamn, Destinee. I'm not sure

what you three were talking about before I came in here, but it almost sounds like you're trying to cover up a murder or something." He chuckled again and waited for the others to join in.

But for obvious reasons they didn't.

His smile faded. "Do I even want to know?"

The three of them shook their heads and responded with various forms of hell no.

"Right." Rex stood and grabbed his coffee. "I think I'm just gonna take this to go then." He nodded gravely and then left the kitchen.

When Jessica heard the front door close, a thought manifested in her mind that never in a million years would she have expected to possess: *What I wouldn't trade to be Coach Rex today.*

Chapter Four

Hiding out was not how Jessica had wanted to spend her first week of summer, but then again, nothing ever went as she thought it would, so there was that.

Destinee's plan, though, had gone off without a hitch. Chris had reported that he hit a hog (his mother was only slightly suspicious about the fact that his truck hadn't been at home for a few days then suddenly he was in a collision), and not a single law enforcement officer had even so much as driven past the McCloud home.

Maybe things would blow over after all.

Jessica pulled the bag of popcorn from the microwave and poured it into a large bowl before bringing it into the living room where her mother was already waiting on the couch with the TV set to the six o'clock news. Her nerves had been in knots since she'd heard about the press conference earlier that morning, and the day had been an exercise in futility as she turned on some oldie-but-goodie nature shows to avoid guessing what in her Father's name Jimmy could be about to say in another damn press conference.

But not even watching predators of Southeast Asia could soothe her anxiety, so when Destinee suggested they make popcorn, drink a beer, and watch the spectacle unfold, Jess decided to just go with it. Besides, her mother was on a roll with plans.

Jessica set the bowl on the couch between them and Destinee handed her a Shiner Bock. "You heard from Maria Flores lately?" she asked.

She had to think about it. "No, not really since the last championship game. Why?"

Destinee shrugged. "Just got this feeling we might need to give her a call soon, is all."

Jess felt a buzzing against her left butt cheek and leaned to the side to pull her phone from her pocket. She had a message from Chris: *Are you watching this? You think it's something political?*

She texted back: *No idea. This is Jimmy we're talking about. It could be anything.*

She set the phone on the couch cushion next to her when suddenly her skull was bombarded for the first time since the accident.

IT'S ALWAYS SOMETHING WITH JIMMY DEAN.
Where have you been?
TURKEY.
Oh. Is that in Asia?
SORT OF. IT'S ASIAN ENOUGH.
What's happening over there?

*MORE LIKE WHAT **ISN'T** HAPPENING OVER THERE. SHEESH.*

What's Jimmy got up his sleeve here?

YOU REALLY WANT TO KNOW?

I thought so, but when you say it like that …

I'LL TELL YOU IF YOU WANT. YOU KNOW I LOVE A GOOD SPOILER.

Will me knowing change anything?

NOPE.

Then tell me.

RUTH WURST.

"Shitballs."

Destinee's head whipped toward her daughter. "What's shitballs, baby?"

But the news anchors had already sent it out to their correspondent on location, and Destinee's attention flickered back and forth between Jess and the television.

"Just watch," she told her mother dejectedly. "You'll see what's shitballs."

Destinee's expression darkened. "Were you just talking with your Father?"

Jessica nodded.

"You do me a favor and ask him to stay the hell outta my relationship with Rex? That shit God pulled last night was *not* okay."

"What shit God pulled—" She cut herself off. First and foremost, she didn't actually want to know how her Father was interfering with Destinee and Rex's sex life. But also, Jimmy approached the microphone to speak.

The media was staged in the parking lot of White Light

Church, which was no surprise. Jimmy had home field advantage there. And it probably didn't hurt that the magnificent arch and statue of him was in frame just above his right shoulder.

"Thank you all for coming," he said, flashing the handsome smile that Jess used to like (and wished she still could). "I want to be clear. I'm here today not as the future mayor of Midland—although I do encourage you to check out my campaign website—but as a humble servant to all the parishioners of White Light Church.

"Last week, one of my most loyal followers was involved in a tragic accident. She's been with the church since it first opened, over a decade ago."

"Fuck me," Destinee breathed. "God dammit. Where's he going with this?"

Jessica shook her head vaguely.

"There are few things in this world that seem magical anymore," Jimmy continued. "As filthy animals, each of us learns to explain away all that magic, all of God's tiny miracles. But today, folks, I come with good news for those of you who don't believe, who ask why we don't see miracles today if God and His only son were able to create them before." He paused, allowing his words to sink in. "And some of you may be saying, 'Nah, Reverend Dean, we've seen a miracle! We've witnessed Jessica McCloud kicking an eighty-yard field goal!'" He chuckled at his exaggerated impression then grinned again. "Right. Sure. The great Lord on high has decided to show Himself through football. Now don't get me wrong, I love football, but that ..." He shook his head quickly. "No, sorry, I don't buy it. No, the Lord Almighty performs *real* miracles, and only for those whom He has chosen. And that's why I'm here today, to present one of those miracles to you in the form of White Light Church's very own Ruth Wurst." He led off the clapping, and overwhelming applause poured from Jessica's television.

"Jesus," her mother said. "There must be all of White Light standing behind the cameras."

Ruth Wurst climbed the three stairs leading onto the small makeshift dais. She smiled and waved enthusiastically, clearly comfortable with her moment in the spotlight. The police chief of Mooretown, Mr. Wurst, followed a few paces behind her. He looked much less enthusiastic about the fanfare, but maybe he was just concerned about his wife.

Mrs. Wurst embraced Jimmy with a hug that lasted just a shade too long and included perhaps an unnecessary amount of body-to-body contact, and Jess swore she saw Chief Wurst's lips tighten as he watched.

Then Mrs. Wurst approached the microphone and Jimmy took a place by her side and a step back, so that real-life Jimmy hovered over one of her shoulders while statue Jimmy hovered over the other. Chief Wurst remained in frame, hovering farther behind his wife, just to the side of statue Jimmy.

"Thank you," Ruth said, smiling and breathing in deeply, her large bosom heaving. "As the great Reverend Dean just said, real miracles are hard to come by nowadays, but I believe that I've experienced one. You see, last Saturday night, I was on my way back to Mooretown from

Midland, where I'd"—she paused for just a millisecond as her eyes flickered down to the podium then back up toward the cameras—"stayed late at White Light Church helping Reverend Dean prepare the troughs for the next day's sacraments. I'd just stopped at a stop sign outside of town, checked both directions, and then proceeded forward when a truck came out of nowhere and T-boned me. The last thing I remember clearly was my head hitting the windshield of my car, and then ... well, it sounds incredible to say, but I died."

She paused just long enough to allow the crowd to gasp and murmur without letting it get out of control. She'd either been coached by the best or this was apparently a role she was born to play.

"I remember seeing a light and hearing God's voice calling me to him. 'Ruth,' He said, 'I've been waiting to welcome you home.' I headed toward that voice, and I just remember the light growing brighter, and my skin started to tingle, almost burning, like I was being purified by His heavenly disdain for my animal instincts and my filth."

Was Mrs. Wurst on the way to heaven?
NO. THE JOURNEY TO HEAVEN IS TOTALLY DIFFERENT. LESS TINGLING, MORE CONFETTI.
So that wasn't you calling to her?
HELL NO.
So if I'd just let her die, she would have gone to ...
HELL, YES.

Jessica wasn't sure how she felt about that. She decided to see how this situation with Ruth played out before she made up her mind.

"But it wasn't my time," Mrs. Wurst began again. "God made that clear when He brought me back. I remember a force flowing through me, like a magnetic pull, drawing me back. And then I opened my eyes ... And that's all I remember."

Jimmy hip checked her away from the mic to take over. "The poor woman was so torn up, she didn't even remember who it was that brought her back. But I do. Because it was *I* who held her crumpled body in my arms and let the good Lord work through me." He held up his hands to calm all the questions that began to rupture from the lips of the reporters.

"It will all become clear to you if you let me explain...

"Ruth had left her bible at the church by accident, and I knew for a fact that she couldn't fall asleep at night without reading her passages and making notes, because that's just the kind of dedicated, unwavering Christian woman that she is. So I headed to Mooretown to drop it off for her so that she could rest well and worship the Lord with all her strength the next day. That's when I saw her car on the side of the road and knew something terrible had happened. The truck that hit her was nowhere to be found, and Mrs. Wurst lay motionless in the brush. I *cried out to God*"—he cried out the words to, presumably, God, but actually just the media—"to save this beautiful and holy woman who had dedicated her life to serving Him, and He heard my prayers." He paused solemnly, letting the emotion of the story hang in a pregnant silence. "I don't know why God chose me to perform His mission, but He did. He most definitely did."

During Jimmy's skewed retelling of events, Jess had kept her attention on Ruth Wurst's face, searching for signs of dissonance. The woman's eyes crossed almost unnoticeably, and Jess figured Jimmy was creating such a fine spectacle that there was a good chance no one but Jess would have noticed the woman's reaction. When he'd mentioned God choosing him, Ruth's upper lip had even twitched, like some mental glitch had occurred in her brain that perhaps even she wasn't aware of. Did she remember Jessica being there? Or did she just *not* remember Jimmy?

"And so," Jimmy continued, "I intend to mete out His justice by bringing whoever committed this horrible hit and run ... to justice. I will not sleep until that person is rotting in a jail cell, sodomized by his or her swinelike equals."

"Jesus fucking Christ, Jimmy," Destinee muttered around a mouthful of popcorn.

"With the help of Mooretown's police chief, Mr. Wurst, who also happens to be a devout member of White Light, each of you watching this, and, of course, the man upstairs, I believe we can find justice for Mrs. Ruth and her family in their difficult time. Chief Wurst will personally oversee this investigation, so please direct any tips to the Mooretown Police Department.

"*Sumus omnes porcos, sed Deus est Aper.* Thank you and have a blessed evening. No questions." He placed his hand on the small of Mrs. Wurst's back and led her toward the edge of the stage. Chief Wurst trailed a few steps behind, still scowling.

And it was done.

Jessica looked over toward her mother, whose mouth dangled open, mashed popcorn visible between her parted lips. Jess hadn't even touched the popcorn yet, and the bowl was almost empty from her mother's nervous eating.

The coverage switched back to the studio, where Chip O'Donnell and Patricia Carrera sat at the anchor desk, seemingly unsure of what to say. Chip swallowed hard, straightened the papers in front of him, then aimed his clear blue eyes at the camera, and plastered on his well-rehearsed smile. "Well that was certainly an interesting development. A miracle in Mooretown."

"*Another* miracle in Mooretown," Patricia added.

"That's certainly what some might say," Chip replied, nodding.

Destinee turned off the TV. "I can't stand their stupid banter. Couple of shit-for-brains idiots."

Jessica suspected her mother didn't always feel so strongly about the news anchors. "So what—" She'd intended to ask, "So what now?" but before she could, her phone vibrated next to her and she knew on instinct who it would be. She didn't bother checking for confirmation before she answered.

"I'm fucked, Jess. My future. It's fucked."

She inhaled deeply. "Relax, Chris. We'll get through this." But she was also feeling the fuckedness. Would God let her rot away in a prison cell? Would He let her be sodomized, whatever that meant? It certainly didn't sound good. Was it a medical procedure? For some reason she thought it was a medical procedure, but she couldn't figure out why they would do that in jail.

"Easy for you to say! You're God's daughter! He wouldn't hang you up to dry. But me? I'm a nobody. He probably doesn't even know my name!"

"Slow down. You're talking crazy. Of course God knows your name. I— I don't know if that's important or not. But listen, we'll figure out something. Just stay where you are. I'll let you know when I have a plan, okay?"

"What if the cops show up at my door?" He started to wheeze. "I just want to play college ball, Jess," he whined. "That's all I want to do."

"I know," she soothed, trying not to roll her eyes. She glanced at Destinee who was staring avidly at her, trying to decipher the conversation. Jessica mouthed "Chris" and Destinee nodded and shoved more popcorn into her mouth. "Would you just do me a favor and check in with Quentin and Miranda? Tell them not to move a muscle until I say. I'll take care of this."

Chris agreed to that but only sounded mildly soothed. Before she hung up, she added, "Maybe try not to sound so terrified when you talk to them."

He agreed to that, too, and she hung up the phone.

YOU KNOW WHAT YOU HAVE TO DO.

I don't actually.

"You got a plan, baby?" Destinee asked.

"Not yet."

"This sounds like something for *your Father* to handle."

"No shit." Jess turned her focus back to Him.

What should I do here?

YOU NEED TO SHUT DOWN JIMMY'S NONSENSE. IT WILL ONLY GET WORSE.

And how do I do that?

THE WORLD NEEDS TO KNOW WHO ACTUALLY FOUND RUTH.

But then the world would also know who killed her. I can't do that to Chris.

THEN DON'T MENTION HIM.

Are you telling me to lie?

NOPE. JUST OMIT. I DO IT ALL THE TIME.

And it's infinitely annoying. But okay. I get what you're saying.

She turned to her mother. "I need a ride down to the station."

"The fuck you say?" Destinee addressed the ceiling next. "That's the best You could come up with? Having our daughter turn herself in?" She shook her head. "So much for that. I got a better idea, baby. *Don't* turn yourself in."

"Mom, this is what I have to do. God's not going to let me rot in jail. Chris's future, Miranda's, Quentin's … I can spare the three of them by taking responsibility."

Destinee's face squished up like she'd tasted something sour. "This reeks of martyrdom to me. I don't like it one bit." She sighed. "But if you're sure this is what you should do, I'll drive you there."

"I'm sure."

"Okay then. Let me put on some pants."

Chapter Five

"I have important information regarding Ruth Wurst's hit and run."

The clerk peered skeptically over the high desk at Jessica, pressing her lips into a tight line. "Why should I believe you when I didn't believe the first hundred people who told me that in the past hour?"

"What?"

The clerk motioned to the waiting room behind Jessica's back, which she'd snaked through only moments before. All the seats were filled and those who weren't lucky enough to secure a chair were packed together, shoulder to shoulder. While Jessica had wondered why so many people would be waiting at a police station, she hadn't been in a state of mind where she was able to put two and two together.

"I guess I don't know why you should believe me. I'm telling the truth?"

The clerk narrowed her eyes. "Wait. Aren't you the

Antichrist girl? You look livelier on TV. Not very threatening at all."

"No, I'm not the … can I please just speak with Chief Wurst?" She'd never imagined confessing to a crime would be this tedious and involve so much persistence.

"Of course you can," the woman replied. "Just gotta wait your turn. Sign in and I'll call you when it's time." She slid a clipboard and pen toward Jessica. A few of the names at the top of the first page had been crossed off, but Jessica had to flip past two more pages before she found an empty line. She sighed but wrote her name and phone number, then headed over to the waiting area to stand as close to a corner as she could.

Once Destinee had found parking in the overcrowded lot, she passed through the automatic glass doors, head swiveling around until her eyes locked onto Jessica's. Then she nodded and made her way through the crowd of people, many of whom stared shamelessly at Jessica but were polite enough not to shout anything horrible.

"You do it?" Destinee whispered.

"Yes."

"And?"

"She doesn't believe me."

Destinee's eyes flew open. "She doesn't believe you?"

Jessica was able to grab her mother's arm and hold her in place before the woman could get two steps toward the clerk's desk. "This probably isn't the best place to cause a scene," Jess hissed.

Her mother narrowed her eyes, but then relaxed and nodded. "Good call. I guess we'll just have to wait."

Gary Higgins sauntered out of a back office, his dark shoulder-length hair greasy as always, with Chief Wurst following a few steps behind him. The chief's upper lip curled slightly, and Jessica recognized that expression because it was the one she wore every time she spoke with Gary or accidentally caught sight of a new busty cat lady he'd drawn.

Gary strutted out of the station like he had just done something heroic, and as he passed her, he nodded. "Hey, Jess. You can go home. I just solved the case."

His voice sent a shudder down her spine, and she didn't bother responding.

Chief Wurst sighed and flipped casually through the list. He had a long night ahead of him for sure, but that didn't necessarily elicit sympathy from Jess, as she had a long night of *waiting* ahead of her, and even once she was done waiting, there was no light at the end of the tunnel. Although considering what she now knew with regards to the light Mrs. Wurst had seen at the end of the tunnel, maybe that wasn't so bad.

The chief stopped skimming over the pages suddenly, and he glanced up until his gaze fell on Jessica. "Ms. McCloud. Follow me."

A few dozen folks who'd been waiting since before Jess arrived grumbled at her preferential treatment, but they didn't warrant any of her sympathy either, considering not a single one had any valuable information on the crime, since none of them had actually been there.

Jessica cut her way through the waiting room crowd and followed Chief Wurst past a row of desks toward the back offices of the station, Destinee lagging only a few steps behind.

For some reason, Jessica had imagined that she would confess inside an interrogation room, but instead he led them to his personal office, closing the door and motioning for them to have a seat on the opposite side of the solid wood desk from himself. It made sense, she supposed. Sure, she'd told the clerk she was there to confess, but the woman didn't exactly believe her and therefore seemed unlikely to pass along the message to the chief.

And now that she was here, with the Mooretown Chief of Police staring at her from only feet away, she wondered for the first time how one started a proper confession. Perhaps style didn't so much matter in this situation.

But before she could speak, Chief Wurst took the lead. "I had a hunch you might pop up in this," he said. He wore a similarly displeased expression to the one he sported at the press conference.

He nodded at Destinee. "Mrs. McCloud."

"Chief Wurst," she said stiffly. Clearly she wasn't sure of the decorum of a confession either. That was oddly comforting, mostly because it meant that maybe Destinee had never found herself in a similar position of guilt before. Though more likely it was because Destinee would never in a million years *willingly* confess anything to the cops.

"What do you have for me, Jessica?" he asked, leaning back slightly in his chair. "Did you see the collision? Did you *cause* the collision? Or did you ... you know." He couldn't say it.

"Resurrect your wife?" She did her best to tamp down

her satisfaction at the discomfort the word *resurrect* seemed to cause him.

"So what is it?" he said curtly. "Don't tell me I let you skip the line just so you can waste my time with made-up heroics or drawings of biped cats with massive tits."

"No, I'm here to confess."

"To?"

It was now or never. "I was driving the truck. But I didn't run the stop sign. Your wife did. She didn't even have her headlights on. She came flying through and clipped the truck and then rolled over into the ditch." She tried to read his expression, but it didn't change, so she continued. "I ran up to her and she was ... dead. And I rolled her over and tried CPR, but as soon as I placed my hand on her chest, she came back to life."

He heaved a deep breath and let it out in a large whoosh as he leaned forward, bracing his elbows on his desk and his chin on his fists. "So Jimmy Dean wasn't there."

"No." Then she remembered who she was talking to and added, "Sir."

"Would you swear it under oath if you had to? That Jimmy Dean wasn't the one who'd performed the miracle?"

"The ... wait. What?" His reaction was *not* matching her expectations. "I was driving Chris's truck. He was asleep and didn't know what happened. I think he was knocked out. He didn't know anything, I told him we'd hit a hog."

He waved her off. "Cut the crap. I don't give a damn about it anyway." He turned toward Destinee, who was strangely silent. "You know about this?"

Destinee raised her jaw, her lips pouting slightly. For a moment it looked like she wouldn't respond, then she spat, "I ain't no snitch."

"Jesus, woman." He turned back to Jessica. "If I helped you write out a confession to all this, would you sign it?"

She was just about to say, "Yes, that's the whole reason why I'm here," but he interrupted before she could. "I mean, of course I would guarantee not to press charges on the hit and run, that's a given. Would you sign it then?"

Again, she was about to say yes before he tacked on, "And obviously Chris wouldn't be facing any charges. And neither would whoever the hell else was in the truck with you on the way back from that sin party over at Brookses' ranch."

Finally, Jessica was allowed to reply. "Yes." But then, "Why would you offer me that?"

"Good question, baby," Destinee added. "Smart."

Chief Wurst nodded. "It's not without a cost. I need something from you."

Uh-oh. That didn't sound good.

*NO, IT'S GREAT. JUST LISTEN. IT'S **HILARIOUS**.*

She ignored God. "And what is that?"

"I need you to hold a press conference."

Jessica groaned. More media attention? "And do what in that conference?"

"In that conference, you will confess to having brought back my wife from the dead."

Then it started to make sense. "Wait, you believe that I did that?"

He shrugged. "Doesn't matter if I do or don't believe

you. What matters is that I don't believe that piece-of-shit false prophet, Jimmy Dean."

"Hot damn," Destinee breathed.

IT GETS BETTER. SERIOUSLY.

"I thought you went to his church," Jessica prodded. "But you don't believe him?"

The chief sucked on his lips, making thoughtful smacking sounds, then he came out with it. "Not since I found out he was *lying* my wife."

"Lying ..." And then it clicked. "You found out about that?!" Jessica yelped.

"Yes. Wait. Did *you* know?" he demanded.

"Well, yeah."

"How?!"

"God told me."

He growled, but didn't say anything disparaging, so Jess would take it.

"Regardless, I trusted him with my family's faith, and it turns out he's no better than the sinners he detests."

You're right. This is great.

She shrugged. "You know what they say. *Sumus omnes porcos* ..."

OHHH SNAP!

No one says that anymore.

SO SAYETH THE LORD.

The chief's face turned plum, but it was clear he needed her too much to say what was on his mind.

Perhaps due to a perverse curiosity about how far she could push him, she added, "It takes a big man to admit he's wrong."

The Chief's left eyelid twitched almost imperceptibly.

"How'd *you* find out?" Jessica added.

Chief Wurst swallowed down his rage, then added, "She told me."

"Damn," Destinee said, her tone hinting the slightest bit at sympathy. "That's cold."

"Yes," he said, sitting up straight. "It was cold. She thought I wouldn't mind because I'd be glad she was alive and had experienced a miracle. But that was ... not the case."

Clearly. "Okay," Jess said, trying not to get too caught up in the unexpected turn this confession had taken. "So if I agree to sign a confession about my miracle and then give a press conference where I tell the world it was actually me who performed the miracle, you'll drop all charges on anyone involved in this accident, even those who you may or may not find out about at a later time?"

He nodded. "That's it."

"And then if I don't agree to your deal ... ?"

"I'll arrest you, Chris, and eventually figure out who else was in the truck—your friend Miranda, I suspect, and then the anonymous report of Ruth's location was traced back to a Darius Jones, who I believe has a son around your age—and I'll make sure they face charges for leaving the scene of the crime as well."

It wasn't much of a decision, then. "Okay, Chief. You have yourself a deal."

Her mother's earlier suspicion was correct, then. She owed Maria Flores a call.

Chapter Six

"You ready?" Chris asked. He'd been noticeably cowed since Jessica had called him and filled him in about her confession. Even though it hadn't turned out terribly for her, he still seemed embarrassed that she'd done it for him.

"As ready as I'll ever be. I mean, it's not like this is the first time I've spoken to the media."

He paused, staring at her meaningfully, as if trying to read her. "Right. But it doesn't always work out well."

Her temper flared suddenly, causing her wonder if it was about to storm above the Mooremont High School parking lot where they'd set the stage for the press conference. "Are you *trying* to freak me out?"

Chris held his hands up in surrender and took a step back. "Sorry. I guess I'm just nervous. I don't particularly trust Mr. Wurst."

"Of course you don't. I don't either."

"It just seems kind of shitty that he would go to all this

trouble to get back at his wife when *he* constantly cheats on *her*."

Jessica nodded. "Yeah, welcome to double standards, Chris." Where was her attitude coming from? She wasn't mad at Chris, and it was in her best interest to keep as many allies as she could.

She peeked out from behind his newly repaired truck, where they'd hidden themselves from the cameras until it was go time.

And it was almost go time. Chief Wurst approached the podium with the Mooretown Police Department shield emblazoned on the front. Mooretown was a quiet place on the whole, yet the chief held himself in front of the cameras like he'd done this a million times, like he was about to announce hit-and-miracle-and-run number twenty-three for the year.

Jessica hoped she could have at least a tiny percentage of the confidence he exuded. She turned back to Chris. "Let's do this."

"Are you mad at me?" Ugh. Why did he think that?

Oh right, the snapping. "No, I'm not." She took a step forward and kissed him quickly before heading out toward the horde, where the Chief had begun briefing the news crews on why he'd called them.

With the media attention facing forward, Jessica was able to mill around behind the crowd and listen to the chief's explanation. Being informed was definitely a good idea, considering she trusted him about as much as she'd trust Jimmy Dean to guard a pot of gold or Emma to go three days without taking a selfie.

"This press conference is in regards to the hit and run incident of which my wife, Ruth Wurst, was recently the victim. This is a follow-up to yesterday's briefing, as more information has since come forward. Some of it fills in the blanks, while some of it contradicts the information that has been previously presented. But I can assure you this is the correct story."

While the reporters didn't say a word, camera shutters clicked and fluttered rapidly, and the small group seemed to undulate like a sea anemone as each shifted restlessly on their feet. Eugene Thornton crouched forward, and he reminded her of an African elephant bull preparing to attack.

"But before we dive into that, I want to make it clear that no charges will be pressed against any known or currently unknown suspects who left the scene of the collision. The Mooretown Police Department has looked into it and found no fault, so there will be no questions regarding that matter."

Jessica's eyes darted over to her mother who stood next to Coach Rex. They hung out off to the side and a little ways behind the media. Coach Rex's arm was draped over Destinee's shoulder as he squinted at Chief Wurst like he was struggling to read an eye chart. Destinee glanced over at her daughter and gave her a hollow thumbs up. Jess sighed deeply. She supposed she should feel relieved that the chief had actually held up his end of the deal, or rather announced it on the record so that she could *hope* he would keep his word. But obviously if he were to renege on his end later on, Jess knew better than to rely on the media to have her back in any meaningful way. Also, it was damn near impossible to feel excited when she still had yet to confess publicly.

No, not confess. That wasn't the right word for announcing you can perform miracles. But it certainly *felt* like the right word.

"As far as new information, it's been discovered that it was in fact the vehicle being operated by Ruth Wurst that ran the stop sign and was driving without headlights at the time, so the fault for the accident does not rest with the other driver."

"Sir, do we know who the other driver was yet?" shouted a female reporter from the throng.

Chief Wurst held up his hand. "I'm getting to that, Julie. Cool it." He cleared his throat. "Yesterday, the driver of the other vehicle came by the office to turn herself in, and in doing so, much more regarding the situation came to light. That's why we're here. I'd like to invite her onto the stage so that you can hear it directly from her. Please refrain from asking questions until the designated time." He peered over the crowd until he spotted Jessica and nodded.

Please don't let me screw this up.

YOU'LL DO FINE. YOU PRACTICED YOUR STATEMENT, RIGHT?

Not really.

OH CHRIST. YOU KNOW YOU'RE NOT GOOD AT IMPROVISING.

And you're not good at helping.

It's a Miracle!

Her feet carried her toward the microphone, even though her mind wasn't present.

WHAT DO YOU SUGGEST I DO TO HELP?

Wha— How am I supposed to know? You're God! You're the man with the plans.

THOU SHALT NOT TAKE THIS THE WRONG WAY, BUT IF YOU EVER REFER TO ME AS A MAN AGAIN, EVEN IN JEST, I WILL SMITE A PUPPY. A CUTE ONE, TOO. NOT ONE OF THOSE HAIRLESS ABOMINATIONS I MADE WHILE I WAS DISTRACTED WITH THE CRUSADES. SECONDLY, HUMANS ARE ESPECIALLY GOOD AT TELLING ME SPECIFICALLY WHAT KIND OF HELP THEY WANT. "GRANT ME THIS," AND "BLESS ME WITH THAT."

Jessica arrived at the edge of the stage.

God hadn't gone on a rant like this is quite some time.

You seem stressed.

God sighed, or at least that's what she thought he did. It felt like steam bellowing from her ears.

IT'S SRI LANKA.

Okay. I don't actually care right now.

BUDDHISTS WERE SUPPOSED TO MAKE MY JOB EASIER—

Seriously, I can't right now.

She arrived at the microphone. And as God continued on about the Buddhists, she employed her only effective strategy to make Him skedaddle. She focused on Eugene Thornton's stupid face with his stupid eyebrows and his stupid mustache and asked herself, *Is Eugene Thornton the Devil?*

The result was inconclusive, but her head was clear.

Chief Wurst had taken a step to the side to give her the floor. The sounds of camera shutters sounded like a swarm of locus wings descending on her. She couldn't deny the satisfaction she felt at having surprised so many of the reporters with her appearance.

Then the beating wings of the cameras started to subside, and it was almost silent. It was definitely time for her to speak. She opened her mouth and the wings flapped frantically again. She shut her mouth. Did they want pictures of her mouth open?

Head in the game, McCloud!

She'd have to pretend this was football. That was the only way she'd be able to keep her mind sharp with this many people watching her.

She opened her mouth again and did a better job of ignoring the fluttering shutters as she tried to remember how she was going to start her statement. Geez, had she not even written talking points on a note card? God was right (as usual); she had done a shit job of preparing. "So yeah," she started off, knowing it wasn't the best lead in. "Um, I was the one driving the vehicle that Ruth Wurst struck the other night. Or I guess it was a week or so ago. But it was still another night."

What am I even saying?

She forged ahead. "She ran the stop sign, like the chief said, and then she clipped the front of my truck. Well, it wasn't my truck, but I was driving it. I don't own a car. Or truck." The sound of cameras had stopped completely, and she thought that wasn't a great sign. Had she confused the photographers into a stupor? Could that be a good strategy? Probably not. "Anyway, that doesn't matter. That's not why I'm here."

"Why *are* you here?" asked a young male reporter, almost pleadingly.

"I'm here because you should know that Jimmy Dean wasn't anywhere near the scene of the accident. And he definitely wasn't the one who brought Mrs. Wurst back to life." She braced herself. "I was. I brought Mrs. Wurst back to life. It was … a miracle." While she'd failed miserably to say the last word with any enthusiasm, it didn't matter, as the reporters went nuts anyway.

"Are you telling me …" Eugene Thornton began.

"Oh Christ," she mumbled on impulse before realizing it might come off as narcissistic.

But it didn't deter Eugene, who pushed ahead with his question. "Let me get this straight, one of your powers as the Antichrist is to bring people back to life?"

Jess rolled her eyes. "I'm not the Antichrist, okay? Jesus. Get it through your head."

Eugene nodded thoughtfully. "You just used the Lord's name in vain. Can you clarify how that doesn't play into the theory that you're the Antichrist?"

"It wasn't the Lord's name. It was His son. They're two very different things."

He was getting her off track. But luckily another familiar voice chimed in to help reel it back. "Miss McCloud," said Maria Flores, brushing gently over the D at the end of her name. "What do you intend to do with your newly discovered miracle of raising the dead?"

They'd discussed this on the phone earlier that morning, but Jessica couldn't for the life of her remember what she was supposed to say. So she opted for, "I plan on raising people from the dead, I guess." She noticed Eugene's eyes light up and knew that wasn't good, so she tried to nip in the bud whatever horrible thing he was thinking that made him grin. "But only good people. Not bringing back any jerks." He was still smiling, and she could only guess at what he was thinking. Whatever it was, she needed to nip *that* in the bud, too. What would be the worst-case scenario of someone bringing a bunch of people back from the dead? Her mind was able to conjure up a visual startlingly quick, and if she hadn't been so hurried to reply, she might have stopped to wonder about it. But Eugene was staring at her eagerly, so she finished with, "And not amassing a loyal army of the resurrected?" The glee on Eugene's face implied that they'd time-hopped to Christmas morning.

*WHAT IN MY NAME WAS THAT? "NOT AMASSING AN ARMY OF THE RESURRECTED?" ME DAMN. THAT'S NOT SUSPICIOUS **AT ALL**.*

I wasn't thinking.

CLEARLY.

What should I do?

STOP TALKING TO ME AND FOCUS, OBVIOUSLY.

Shit!

She'd spaced out in front of everyone. This was not good.

Reporters were shouting all kinds of absurd questions now, like, "Are you having a stroke?" and "Will there be death panels that decide who the real jerks are?" and "Will your army of undead include illegal immigrants?"

Maria was waving at her. She looked at the woman, who mouthed, "No more questions."

Yeah, that seemed like a good idea. "No more questions," she said, and then she sprinted from the staging area, making a beeline for Chris's truck.

Chris was a step ahead, and by the time she reached the F-350, the engine was already thrumming and Chris waited in the driver's seat. She climbed in and didn't need to say a word. He hauled ass out of the school parking lot.

It wasn't until they were a mile down the road when she realized that maybe, just maybe, fleeing from a press conference wouldn't do much for her public image.

* * *

Only half a mile down the road from Mooremont, Jess answered her phone. Maria shouted to be heard over the ruckus of the staging area. "Gordon's," she managed. "Be there in fifteen. Someone I want you to meet."

After agreeing, Jessica hung up the phone. A burger sounded nice anyway, so she told Chris the new plan and he gladly took the necessary detour and headed to Gordon's instead of the McCloud home.

They already had their food and Chris had just stood from their booth to refill his soda when Jessica saw Maria enter with a woman she'd never seen before.

Gordon's was always busy over the summer, but all

activity ceased as soon as Maria and the other woman walked in, their curves anything but hidden away in the flattering, high-quality, form-fitting clothes that Jess was sure couldn't have been bought at any local stores. Maria's friend didn't seem to mind the attention, and Jessica hoped the woman assumed the stares were because she was a bombshell and not because she was black. Although after the eye-opening few months of having dated a black guy, Jessica knew that realistically both factors were equally likely culprits.

Maria spotted Jessica and waved, and the two ladies crossed the dining room, stopping at the edge of the table. "Jessica, I'd like for you to meet Wendy Peterman."

Jessica stood as much as she could in the cramped booth and shook hands with the woman. "Nice to meet you."

"Pleasure's mine," said Wendy. Her voice was smooth and warm, and Jessica liked her immediately.

"Y'all are welcome to sit," she said, motioning to the bench across from her. "Or, I guess you might want to get food first."

"Maybe later," Maria added before sliding into the booth, only experiencing minor difficulty in keeping her A-line skirt in a modest position as she scooted over to make room for Wendy. Wendy's slick pants allowed her to sit gracefully a moment before Chris reappeared at the table. He plopped down next to Jessica and looked over at Wendy. "Chris."

"Ah yes, I've heard about you from Maria." She nodded in a way that assured him it was all good things.

Chris's eyes remained shamelessly glued to Wendy,

even as she turned her attention to Jessica and Maria began a more comprehensive introduction. "Wendy is a PR specialist out of Dallas."

"PR?" Jessica asked.

"Public relations," Wendy said. "I work predominantly with individuals as opposed to corporations or small businesses."

"And what do you do exactly?" Jessica asked, already sure that any job that allowed Wendy to buy the clothes she wore, maintain the expensive manicure, and afford housing in Dallas was one Destinee wouldn't be able to pay her to do.

"I help high profile individuals manage their public image. Help empower them to take control of the narrative of their lives."

"And she's *very* good at it." Maria added. "I called her yesterday to come down for the press conference to see if you were a client she might be interested in working with."

Jessica's stomach dropped. "You were there for the press conference?"

Wendy pressed her lips together and nodded almost imperceptibly. "Yes. Not great, but salvageable." She paused, then folded her fingers together on the table. "I'll be honest with you, Jessica, I've been following your story from the start. And you've botched almost every opportunity for positive coverage."

When Jess noticed her mouth was hanging open, she wondered how long it'd been that way. No one had ever been so frank with her, and while she could feel her face turning red at the brutal assessment, she also knew

Wendy was entirely correct. "Yeah, this isn't my strong point."

"I'm glad you realize that," Wendy added. "It means you'd be a dream client." She smiled, and Jessica felt an instant pang of guilt, knowing she would have to refuse the woman's help. She couldn't ask Destinee to work more hours than she already was, and once football season started, Jessica wouldn't have a single second to spare for a job between athletics and school. And then there was the whole thing of her senior year approaching. When adults mentioned senior year, they had a tendency to draw out the word, lower their voice and raise their eyebrows significantly to convey, she supposed, the gravity of such a rite of passage.

It was almost as if Maria could sense Jessica's hesitancy, because she began to sweeten the pot. "Wendy represents some of the hottest public figures right now. Jeremy Divorak, Cherry Valencia," she paused, then added, "Jameson Fractal."

Jessica's eyes darted to Wendy. "You represent Jameson Fractal?"

Wendy bit back a laugh. "Yes. Although that's a recent development. But yes, he's one of my clients."

Vague possibilities of being in the same place at the same time as her long-time celebrity obsession began to swirl in a foggy stew in her mind and her heart began to race. Then she reminded herself that Wendy's connection to Jameson didn't matter, really; Wendy was out of the McCloud price range.

Being poor sucked.

"I just don't know if I can." she said, before sucking her Dr. Pepper morosely through her straw.

"And why's that?" Wendy asked.

"Yeah, why's that?" Chris echoed.

She glanced at him. Did he have to be so obvious? She couldn't blame him for his attraction, she supposed, considering *she* was having a hard enough time taking her eyes off the woman's delicate yet fierce features, and holy crap did anyone naturally have such perfect, round, perky breasts, or was that a bra thing, and if it was a bra thing, where could Jessica buy that bra?

She reeled in her thoughts. "We're just not in a place where we could afford that sort of thing, I don't think."

"Oh no," Wendy said quickly, as she leaned over the table and placed a soft hand on Jessica's wrist. "I wouldn't charge you."

"Huh?"

Wendy leaned back and chuckled good-naturedly. "Listen, I'm a business woman through and through, but I'd have to be out of my mind to charge God's only daughter for PR work."

Again, Jess said, "Huh?" Then it sunk in. "Wait, you believe in me?"

"Of course, dear. There's no way you could know this about me, but usually I'm the kind of person that people seek out, not the other way around. If I thought you were anything other than God's daughter, I would *not* drive all the way from Dallas to this time capsule of a town—where legalized slavery is probably still on the books—to offer you my services." She laughed, and Jess laughed along with her, though it was mostly forced.

"Yeah, I guess that wouldn't make sense." *Kind of like this whole conversation.*

Wendy leaned back in her seat and looked at the shiny gold watch on her wrist. "Well, listen, I do need to get back to Dallas before traffic sets in. You don't have to give me a yes or no right away, but promise me you'll think about it, talk it over with your mom or whoever else you trust, and then give me a call one way or another."

Jessica nodded and Wendy reached in her pocket and pulled out a business card. "My cell number is written on the back. Call that, not my office. You'll never get past the centurion of a receptionist I hired." She smiled again and then stood. Maria scooted out as well.

"Promise you'll call?" Wendy urged.

The reality of free help was starting to settle in, and Jessica was reminded of the weightless sensation of taking off her sweaty football pads and helmet after a late-summer game. "Yes. Definitely."

"Wonderful." She turned to Chris. "It was a pleasure meeting you, Christopher."

He muttered something back that sounded like, "Amb atchoo," and the two women left Gordon's.

"I think she seems trustworthy," he said, once he regained the ability to speak real words.

Jessica rolled her eyes. "Of course you do."

Chapter Seven

It wasn't until the previous Tuesday that Jessica had begun to wonder if she should say something, like a catch phrase, each time she brought patients back to life, and now it was almost all she could think about, as the fifty-four-year-old shooting victim on the table in front of her breathed the first breath of his second chance at life.

That's the stuff!

No, that was a terrible catch phrase. Almost as bad as the others she'd thought of that morning while miracling the patients of Midland Memorial Hospital, like *Back in the game!* and *Round two!* and *Don't go toward the light!*

The last one was only *sort* of a joke, considering what she knew about that light, knowledge she'd long since decided to keep to herself. Maybe someday she would mention it to those closest to her in passing, like, "Hey, if you ever die and see a bright light … Just maybe pass on it," or "You know what would be a good idea if you die?

Going toward the confetti. I bet that's Heaven. What? No reason."

On the table, the man's wounds were nearly closed up and he opened his eyes with the blankness and disappointment of one who'd thought it was time for dessert, only to discover this was a fourteen-course vegan meal and he was still on the first of many tofu courses.

He was the last patient in need of her miracles after a long morning shift, and she was ready to move on to something else, maybe some ice cream, a few episodes of classic David Attenborough narration, maybe a good makeout sesh with Chris.

Once the bullets finally surfaced from the man's open wounds (she'd never get used to the squelching pop it made), the nurses helped him sit up and began explaining to him what in God's name, literally, had just happened to him. Jess wondered if he was a jerk. She'd promised not to bring back jerks, but it was always hard to tell once they were dead and she couldn't have a real conversation with them. And of course everyone was always viewed as a saint immediately following their death, so talking with the patient's family was never much use. They were *all* good, hard-working fathers, mothers, daughters, uncles who did the best they could until they were gunned down by a rival gang or drove their car—accidentally?—off an overpass with all their kids inside.

Anyway, there was no telling. She'd lost count of how many people she'd brought back to life once she hopped into triple digits. And that was all within the first week. Why were so many people terrible at the simple act of not dying? She was only ever brought the untimely deaths, so perhaps that skewed her perspective slightly, but after a few repeat customers, she started to become a cynic. When she'd mentioned it to Wendy, the woman's response had simply been, "Well, no one likes their first job."

Jess thought she might like it a lot more if she were getting paid, but this wasn't that sort of a setup, Wendy had explained. "Think of it as an unpaid internship. Your reward is the knowledge that you're helping people." It wasn't all that rewarding.

"Confetti …" mumbled the man sitting on the table in front of her.

"Huh?" asked one of the nurses. "Sir. Do you remember your name?"

"Confetti!" he shouted more adamantly.

Another nurse turned to Jessica. "What's he saying?"

Jess shrugged. "You know how they get sometimes. Anyway, I got to go." At least she was able to end the day on a high note, knowing that perhaps one of her patients wasn't a complete jerk.

She washed her hands in the sink, then pulled out her phone and texted Wendy to let her know another day of her unpaid summer internship had gone off without a hitch. Then Jessica made her way out of her private room in a mostly vacant wing of the hospital, down the hall, and toward the elevator.

"See ya tomorrow," hollered Julian, one of the many orderlies she'd befriended during her month at Midland Memorial. She waved without looking up from her phone.

The elevator doors were already closing in front of her

when she glanced up to press the button for the ground floor and finally noticed who was standing next to her in the enclosed space. "Dr. Fractal?"

The woman, who also had her head in her phone, glanced up and her eyes opened wide when she saw who was speaking to her. "Jessica."

"You know my name?"

The doctor slipped her phone into the large pocket of her white coat and nodded as the elevator began its descent with a small jolt. "Of course. Everyone knows your name around here."

"Oh right."

"But I do also remember you from Marymoore." She beamed. "That was quite a memorable day."

Jessica shuddered. "Yeah, it was."

The doors opened onto the lobby and both the elevator occupants stepped out. Jess paused, assuming it was time for them to part ways, since she was headed straight to the front doors, and she didn't figure Dr. Fractal was done for the day, but before she could say her farewells, Dr. Fractal took a step closer to her, leaned in, and said, "Listen, what you're doing here each day, it's been really hush hush. I get that. And if you're doing what I suspect you're doing, I understand why it would be in the best interest of everyone working here and visiting here for it to *not* become public knowledge. But I have to know." She paused and placed her arm on Jessica's shoulder to move her out of the path of an oncoming gurney, then leaned in close again. "As the chief of obstetrics and gynecology here, I know better than anyone that once in a blue moon something happens and we lose a patient. We lost one last week. I was called into the room right after it was confirmed and saw it. Then I saw that same patient walk out of this lobby we're standing in, right here, later that afternoon. And then an hour later, I saw you walk out of this lobby." She paused. "Am I getting it right? Is that what you're doing here?"

Wendy had been clear in her directions not to tell anyone she didn't have to about why she had a private room in a mostly empty wing of the hospital. But this was Dr. Fractal. She was solid. And she'd guessed it anyway.

So Jess nodded. "Yeah, that's what I'm doing here."

The doctor worried her lip, her eyebrows crowding in toward the bridge of her nose as she nodded slightly. "Good," she said finally. "Thank you. And thank you for keeping it quiet." She looked up and her expression cleared. "I'll let you go enjoy your summer, then."

"See you tomorrow," Jessica said.

Dr. Fractal chuckled airily. "Yes, see you tomorrow."

She texted Miranda only to find that her friend was already waiting in the parking lot. It was normally Chris who picked her up from her summer internship and drove her the forty-five minutes home from Midland, but he'd called the night before to say he had something come up (he was vague on *what* had come up, but Jessica figured it was likely another college-related task his mother had set out for him, meaning he wasn't actually sure what it was himself) and Miranda had been an easy choice for back up. With the hiding out and whirlwind of the past month and a half since school let out, she'd hardly been able to spend more than a few minutes with her best friend.

Cheyenne Forte's Corolla pulled around to the patient pick-up circle and Jess hopped in.

"Happy birthday," Miranda said, once Jess had shut the door. "You thought I forgot."

Jessica giggled. "I didn't think you forgot."

"Good, because I didn't."

Jessica wasn't sorry to leave the hospital behind today. It hadn't been an especially busy Thursday, but that didn't mean it was slow. She'd thought about calling in sick when she'd woken up groggy and with a slight sinus headache. Of course that would've meant the four people she resurrected (with whom she now shared a birthday of sorts) wouldn't have survived the day. It was that thought that got her out of bed every morning when she just as easily could've slept in and enjoyed her summer like most kids her age, because calling in sick was a decision to let people die, and who was she to play God, really?

Well.

"You know, if you'd just told Chris it was your birthday, I bet he wouldn't have canceled on you."

She waved her friend off. "But it doesn't matter, because I don't celebrate it."

"But still. Don't you think he'd like to know?"

"Probably, but it's not his choice. He's only asked once and he understood why I didn't tell him. It's not even an exciting one. Nobody cares about seventeen."

Miranda wiggled slowly in her seat while she replied in a mischievous tone, "Age of consent in Texas ..."

"Consent for what?" When Miranda gave her an oh-come-on look, Jess thought harder about it. "Oh. Sex. Yeah, I guess it is. Not like I'm taking advantage of it."

"Really? Still not?"

Jessica shrugged. "No. I just don't want to yet."

"You don't want to or you don't want to with *him*?"

"I don't want to with anyone."

Miranda hesitated, then said, "It's really not that bad."

"Yeah, probably—wait! What?" Jessica nearly gave herself whiplash with how quickly her head turned to look at her best friend, who was expertly holding back a mischievous grin. "What?!"

"What?"

"What do you mean, what? When did this happen?" Jessica realized she was shouting and tried to take it down a notch.

Miranda just laughed. "Last week."

"Last week?!" Not that there was anything particularly special about last week, but it still seemed ludicrous anyway. "With who, Lewis? Are y'all back together?"

Miranda fake gagged. "Ew. No, not Lewis."

"Wait. Quentin?!" Jessica gave up on controlling her volume. She'd been blindsided, and she felt as if she were slipping and sliding on ice, trying to get her feet back under her again.

Miranda nodded. "Yeah, Quentin."

"Quentin!" Jess threw her hands into the air. "You had sex with Quentin!"

Miranda was kind enough not to say anything else until Jess digested the new bit of information. Then finally, once her brain had stopped spinning, she was able to speak at a normal volume. "So how was it?"

Miranda shrugged. "It was okay."

"Did you, you know ... orgasm?"

"Psh. Of course not. The whole thing lasted like five seconds."

While Jessica was no expert, that seemed a little quick. "Do you regret it?"

Miranda glanced in the rearview mirror and narrowed her eyes at something as she replied distractedly, "Not at all. Glad I got it out of the way, actually." She looked at Jess. "Sorry I didn't tell you right away. I wanted to tell you in person, and this is sort of the first chance ..."

"Yeah, sorry. You know I suck at balancing my miracles with, well, with anything else."

"Yeah," Miranda said airily, and when Jessica looked at her, she realized Miranda wasn't actually paying attention. Instead, her focus had returned to her rearview mirror.

"What is it?" Jessica asked.

Miranda shook her head and refocused on the road. "No, nothing. Just the person behind us was ... I dunno. Sorry, what were you saying?"

"It doesn't matter," Jessica said. "I want to hear about you and Quentin. Are y'all a thing? What happens when he leaves for college? Are you gonna have sex with him again?"

Miranda blushed and laughed, and then dove into the juicy details, most of which Jess immediately wished she hadn't asked about.

They were only a few miles outside of Mooretown when

Miranda interrupted herself midway through a quite graphic and detailed description of the moment of penetration to say, "You know, I don't want to sound paranoid, but this same car has followed us all the way from Midland Memorial."

"What?" Jess turned in her seat to look back at the car behind them.

"Do you recognize them?" Miranda asked.

Squinting to see through the glare from the late afternoon sun on their windshield, Jess tried to make out any defining features of the driver. "No."

"A reporter, maybe?"

Jess shook her head. "None I've met before. And I've met a lot of them. Also, I don't know any with a Mexico license plate."

"Could it just be a coincidence?" Miranda asked hopefully, though she didn't sound convinced of the possibility.

Jess knew better than to hope for coincidences in her life. "I doubt it."

"I mean, it's probably nothing dangerous, right?" Miranda asked. "God keeps you pretty safe."

"Right. Of course." She decided not to add that He made no promises for Jessica's loved ones.

The sex talk was dead in the water as a heavy silence took up most of the space inside the Corolla.

As they passed the sign for Mooretown city limits, Miranda asked, "Should we head somewhere else? If we're being followed, we don't want to lead them to your house."

"Good idea."

"Where should we go then?"

"The police station?"

Miranda thought about it, then said, "Yeah, I guess that works."

They drove past the turn for Jessica's neighborhood and turned a quarter mile further down, onto the street that led to the police station.

The car that had followed them from the hospital didn't turn, but kept on driving. Jessica tried to get a better look at the driver and spied a middle-aged Hispanic woman driving with a younger Hispanic male—possible her son or maybe a younger brother or, hell, a young lover—asleep in the back seat.

"So maybe it *was* just a coincidence," she muttered. "Huh." First time for everything, she supposed. But her hackles didn't go down.

Miranda executed a tight U-turn and headed back toward Jessica's house.

Once they'd pulled into the driveway, Jessica invited Miranda inside to cool off with some of the massive cache of peanut butter cup ice cream she'd spotted in the freezer that morning. Miranda was more than willing to partake.

But as soon as Jess stepped out of the car and closed the door, her brain, still on high alert, registered the sound of another vehicle driving down the street toward them, and she glanced up, already knowing what she'd see. "Shit. Miranda. It's that car."

Miranda's doe eyes became large saucers. "That can't be good. Get inside."

Jess didn't have to be told twice. She didn't want to run, though—for predators, that was the wrong choice in the fight or flight response—so she began power walking toward the front door as if all the natural alarms in her body weren't blaring.

The front tire of the car hopped the curb a moment after the brakes screeched, and before it had even come to a complete stop, the woman jumped out from the driver's seat and began yelling frantically in Spanish. "*¡Espera! ¡No te vayas! ¡Ayúdame! ¡Ten piedad, por favor!*"

"Come on!" Miranda yelled.

But Jessica stopped in her tracks. The woman was panicked and loud, sure, but she didn't seem like a threat. Maybe she just needed help.

Then a second later, the woman flung open the back door, reached in, and pulled out a limp body.

"Jess! Come on!" Miranda yelled again.

The woman continued to holler and plead as she strained to drag the young man's body up the driveway toward Jessica. "*¡Por favor! ¡Sólo tú puedes ayudarle! ¡Por favor, ten piedad, Yesica Crista!*"

Now that he was out of the car, Jessica realized that he was not, in fact, sleeping. Holy hell, the body was in bad shape. Jessica scrunched up her nose as she took a closer look at the thing. She felt Miranda's hand touch her arm, but then the girl paused as she caught sight of the corpse in the begging woman's arms. "Holy shit. What happened to him?" she said, apparently forgetting all about running.

The woman dropped the body facedown at Jessica's feet and started jabbering on again. "*¡Tienes que ayudarle! ¡Te suplico! ¡Es mi jovencito, y no le puedo perder!*"

"Jesus Christ," Jessica breathed. She couldn't tear her eyes from the horror of the corpse.

"Are those *all* bullet holes?" Miranda asked, quietly.

Jessica shook her head vaguely. "It's like the bullet holes have bullet holes."

"Did he get shot and *then* drown, you think?"

The woman leaned down and used her arms as levers to roll the young man closer toward Jessica, who had to take a step back to keep the bloated body from landing on her tennis shoes. The movement caused an overwhelming foul smell to escape the body, and Jess struggled to hold back the vomit that started creeping up her esophagus. It didn't seem very godly to vomit on a corpse she was supposed to resurrect.

"*¡Mijo!*" The woman was crying now. "*¡Por favor, ayúdale!*"

"Oh," Miranda said. "It's her son. I remember that from Spanish class."

Jessica had taken three years of Spanish in junior high, too, but nothing about this situation made any more sense because of it.

The woman lunged forward and fell onto her knees, tugging at the waist of Jessica's shirt. "*¡Por favor, Mija Divina!*"

The contact pulled Jessica from her stupor and time seemed to resume its normal speed. She nodded down at the woman. "Okay. Yeah. Si."

"*¿Sí, me ayudarás? ¡Ay, gracias a Dios!*" The woman let go of Jessica's clothing and stepped back to wait for the miracle.

This seems ill advised. She'd never brought back someone who was this bad off or had been dead for as long as this young man clearly had. But a miracle was a miracle, right?

She crouched next to the body just as she heard the front door open behind her and turned to see Chris step out.

"What are *you* doing here?" she asked. She hadn't seen his truck anywhere when they'd pulled up.

"What's going on?" he asked, taking in the situation quickly as he approached.

Jessica moved to the side so he could get an eyeful of the bloated, riddled, water-logged body piled in a heap in the driveway.

He jumped back and shielded his eyes. "Oh fucking hell!"

"¿¡Vas a ayudarle o no?!" yelled the woman impatiently.

Chris's horror only intensified after hearing the Spanish. "What'd she say?"

"I think she wants Jess's help," Miranda replied.

Destinee and Rex hustled out the front door then. Destinee was the first to notice the strangers. "What the fucking shit?"

Jess opened her mouth to explain, but clearly the desperate woman was done waiting and grabbed at Jess's shirt again, shouting, *"¡Basta! ¡Resucitale de la muerte, ya!"*

Destinee charged forward. "You lay one more hand on my baby and I'll—"

But Miranda stepped forward and held Destinee back with her shockingly strong softball arms. "It's fine. She just wants help for her kid."

Destinee stopped struggling, but didn't look happy about it.

Jess swatted the woman's hands from her shirt. "All right already. He's not getting any deader ..." She knelt down next to the body, and whether everyone had fallen silent or her mind had blocked out all the voices around her, she couldn't be sure.

Do I really have to touch this guy?

There had to be two dozen bullet holes in his chest alone, and his face was blue and white, puffy in some places, skin dissolved from others.

What the hell happened to you? She had a sneaking suspicion that he might've been a real jerk before he was killed. Rarely did nice people end up with *this* many bullets. It seemed like a waste of good ammunition unless the people who did this really hated him and added the last dozen into the mix for gratification. But it wasn't up to her to judge. It was all conjecture anyway. And there was just no way this woman would leave if Jessica refused to give her what she wanted.

She leaned forward, making sure to mouth breathe, and touched her hand to his heart. Even with the light pressure, there was a squelching sound that jump-started her gag reflex. She closed her eyes to steady herself and felt the magnetism pulse from her torso out through her arms and then into the young man on the ground in front of her. He jolted but then was still.

Shit, did it not work? Had she just discovered the limitation of her miracle?

She held her breath and was about to try again, when

It's a Miracle!

his eyelids opened and one watery eye stared back at her. Where the other eye should have been was just an empty socket.

Shitballs. What happened to his—

The screaming that erupted from him was like nothing she'd ever heard before. Hoarse, primal, loud as a police siren—the noise caused her to jump back from him quickly, and she fell onto her ass before hurriedly scooting away.

If you could boil agony down to its purist form, it would sound a little like the screams coming from the resurrected one-eyed man in front of her.

And then his mother began screaming, sheer panic, which sounded the same in Spanish as it did in English.

"Holy shit!" Jess yelled. "Someone call 9-1-1!"

Chris ran to her and pulled her to her feet as Miranda hollered, "What do we do?!"

The body writhed on the ground, gurgling and hacking sounds occasionally mingling with his screams.

What neighbors were home at this time on a Thursday were out on their porches now, though none seemed in a hurry to do anything helpful.

"Rex, get my gun," hollered Destinee.

Jess turned toward her mother. "Mom, no! You don't get to just kill him again!"

"You want me to leave him like this?" she demanded frantically.

The woman was in a heap on the ground next to her son, crying and trying to comfort him as he continued to choke on his screams. She looked up toward Jessica. *"Agua! Agua, por favor!"*

"Is someone calling 9-1-1?" Jess yelled, looking toward Miranda, then Chris, then Rex and Destinee. No one was. "Someone call 9-1-1!"

The screaming and gurgling intensified. "And someone get him some water!"

As Miranda fumbled with her phone and Rex ran inside, hopefully to get water rather than to fetch Destinee's gun, Jessica thought, *This is a nightmare, right? This is just a nightmare.*

NIGHTMARISH, YES, BUT NO NIGHTMARE.

God! Help! What do I do?

YOU SHOULDN'T HAVE BROUGHT THIS ONE BACK.

Well no shit.

MANKIND, THIS IS JUST A BAD DEAL ALL AROUND.

She looked down at the body that was still screaming and flopping in its mother's arms as the woman wept with horror.

YOU OUGHT TO PUT HIM OUT OF HIS MISERY.

Are you really telling me to kill him right after I brought him back?!

IT WOULD BE THE MERCIFUL THING TO DO.

He's not just some wounded animal!

WELL.

Okay, but he's a human *animal. Isn't all human life precious?*

SURE. WHATEVER. BUT LOOK AT HIM. I MEAN ... YUCK.

Rex ran back out of the house, and Jess found herself slightly disappointed to see that he'd opted for the glass of water. He handed it to the mother, who poured it into her son's mouth as her blubbering quieted momentarily. He gagged and when she rolled him over onto his side, he began vomiting, load after load.

"God dammit!" Jess said, turning away.

"EMS is on its way," Miranda announced, pocketing her phone again.

There was nothing to do but wait for the ambulance to show up then and hope that maybe in the meantime the young man died on his own, which really meant she hoped God did the necessary dirty work.

Chris kept his arm around Jessica for as long as he could until he was forced to jet to the side of the driveway to begin vomiting violently. When Miranda looked over and caught sight of him, the last tenuous thread of her control snapped, too, and she ran to the opposite side of the pavement to let loose the contents of her stomach, leaving Jessica standing alone while her best friends spewed in synchronicity with the resurrected monstrosity until finally, after what seemed like an eternity, the ambulance arrived.

"What the hell happened?" begged one of the EMTs as he absorbed the scene. He leaned forward to grab the body and move it to the gurney, but when he caught of whiff of the writhing bloated man, he jumped back like he'd been punched in the face. "Oh lord have mercy."

I'M SERIOUSLY CONSIDERING IT.

The other EMT, a woman, began speaking Spanish to the inconsolable woman, and as she asked more and more questions, her face turned to one of disbelief and her eyes darted toward Jessica more than a few times.

"I was just trying to help," Jessica whimpered, stepping

back to allow the first responders plenty of room (and because she was *so* done with this whole scene).

With his stomach empty, Chris returned to her side and wrapped a shaking arm around her shoulder. As the EMTs loaded the screaming body onto the gurney and lifted it on the count of three, Jessica had the foolish thought, *At least it's almost over.*

And that's when she saw the news van fly around the corner and onto her street.

No. It can't be. Not him.

Despite his soft, unathletic frame, Eugene Thornton could hustle when he needed to, and the front tire of the Channel Six van hopped the curb only a moment before coming to a sudden stop so that the news crew could jump out, camera already rolling.

How did he know to come here?

Then it occurred to her: *Is Eugene Thornton the Devil?*

The Devil Test results were, of course, inconclusive. But she suspected that the Devil wouldn't be as openly unabashed as Eugene was about the level of enjoyment ruining lives brought him.

"Rex, I ain't playing this time," Destinee said. "Go get my gun."

"We better get inside," Chris said. "Wendy's going to be pissed when she hears about this." He tried to lead Jessica away, his arm still around her shoulder, and as much as she wanted to leave all this behind, preferably locking it away in a tiny box inside a safe inside a vault inside the darkest cavern of her mind, she couldn't go yet. Not until she saw it through. Once the body was loaded up and the ambulance pulled away, then she could head inside, but not before.

Thankfully, Eugene seemed more interested in getting shots of the body and the screaming Mexican woman than he did in hammering Jess with questions.

Or at least he did at first. But once the ambulance doors closed, he didn't miss a beat before turning and jogging toward her. "Ms. McCloud! Ms. McCloud! A few questions about the writhing man in your driveway."

"Yep, time to go." She let Chris herd her toward the front door, and she followed Miranda, who was also jogging toward safety.

"No comment," Chris hollered over his shoulder as the reporter gained on them.

When Jessica reached the doorstep, though, she stopped in her tracks. "What the hell?"

As she gazed inside the house, she realized that some major redecoration had taken place in the time between when her mother drove her to Midland Memorial that morning and when she'd arrived home.

Perhaps because she'd never been the recipient of decorations like this before, it took a minute for the "Happy Birthday Jessica!" banner and the bunches of helium-filled balloons and the triple-decker cake with a 1 and a 7 candle on the top to any make sense.

Destinee, whose orders were not being followed by her boyfriend and had therefore taken matters into her own hands, rounded the corner from the hall with a shotgun on her hip. She paused when she saw Jessica staring. "Oh, surprise, baby." Then she charged past her daughter, out the door, and started hollering for Eugene to get off her property.

Chris hurried Jess the rest of the way inside as Eugene chuckled behind her, "You think this is the first time someone's pointed one of those at me?"

The last thing Jess heard before Destinee backed up into the house and slammed the door was likely the only thing that that could have made a bad day worse.

"A breaking discovery at the McCloud home," Eugene said excitedly. "We've just discovered that today, July seventh, is the birthday of Jessica McCloud, who some call the Mooretown Messiah."

Jessica wondered if the string of profanities her mother shouted was enough to keep the audio clip from being usable. But it didn't matter. Eugene could re-record it. And he would if he needed to, because he'd just hit the gold mine.

Jessica walked straight to the couch, moved a wrapped gift out of the way, and then flopped facedown onto the plastic-covered cushions.

Miranda sat down on the floor next to the couch right by Jessica's head. "That was messed up."

Jess nodded, her nose squeaking against the clear plastic. She turned onto her side to face her friend. "I shouldn't have brought him back."

"Don't beat yourself up, baby," Destinee said after setting down the shotgun. "You couldn'ta known."

Jess huffed and propped herself up on her elbow. "Did you *see* him? Maybe I couldn't have *known*, but I definitely could've guessed. Guy was seriously mangled."

"FUBAR," Coach Rex muttered from his place between the TV and cake. When the others turned to look at him, he added, "That's what we called it in Iraq. It stands for ... well"—he looked around the room at the teenagers and reconsidered—"it's probably not appropriate—"

"Fuck, Rex, what're you going on about?" Destinee interrupted. She waved him off. "Doesn't matter. Listen, Jess. Forget all that. It's your birthday. Let's celebrate. How 'bout some cake?"

The idea of eating didn't sound particularly appetizing after all the vomiting she'd just witnessed. "I'm good. Y'all can get at it."

Destinee looked to Miranda, who grimaced and shook her head, then to Chris who hesitated but nodded. "Yes, please."

"Do you want us to sing happy birthday first?" Destinee asked.

Jess leaned forward, arms braced on her knees, and pinched the bridge of her nose to stave off a tension headache she felt setting in. "Please don't."

And so Destinee went ahead and pulled the candles out of the cake and lit them before bringing them to where Jessica clearly wasn't getting up from the couch. "Make a wish, baby."

I wish I couldn't perform miracles.

NICE TRY.

Through gritted teeth, Jessica blew out the candles.

Chapter Eight

"Sounds like you're relieved to be back in school, then," Mrs. Thomas said from her large office chair at Mooremont High. It'd taken a solid half hour of non-stop storytelling for Jessica to catch up Mrs. Thomas on all the gory details of her summer, but the effort was well worth it, as Jess took a deep breath, felt the muscles in her chest and back relax, and melted into the love seat nestled in the corner of her principal's cozy office.

"You know, Mrs. Thomas? I actually kind of am. I never thought I'd say that."

Mrs. Thomas laughed. Jessica always thought the woman's laugh sounded like a cherry blossom smells. "And to make good news better, it's your senior year, which is always the easiest for students like you, who chose to get so much of the hard work out of the way last year."

"I thought it was supposed to be the hardest," she said. "That's what everyone always says." She was pretty sure

Mrs. Thomas had even said it a handful of times, but she didn't mention that.

"It can be the most stressful for some, sure, because of the pressure of selecting a college, the SATs, getting used to the idea of leaving your home behind and starting out on your own life where you're the only one responsible for yourself …"

Jessica's shoulders clenched. "I guess I haven't really thought about all those things."

Mrs. Thomas pressed her lips together, shook her head, and swiped at the air between them. "Oh no, there's no need to worry. There are plenty of students who I *do* worry about in that regard, but you're not one of them. You're level-headed, competent, a hard worker, all the things colleges drool over. And the great thing about a town like Mooretown is that you can leave for years at a time, and when you come home, nothing's changed." She chuckled lightly, and Jess felt like she was missing the joke, but she chuckled along anyway. "You'll be fine. One step at a time. It's only your first week back, so you have months to decide what college best suits you. And you know I'll write you a glowing letter of recommendation when that time comes."

"Thanks." Jess glanced up at the clock on the wall. "Speaking of which, I need to head over to my first college counseling meeting."

Mrs. Thomas beamed. "Oh wonderful! Tell Brian I said hello!"

Jess nodded. "Sure thing." Though it didn't make much sense to her why she would pass along such a message when the two of them had offices only yards away from one another.

"Anyway, I don't want to keep you," continued Mrs. Thomas, "but thank you for stopping by. I've been meaning to check in with you all summer, see how things were going with you and your highly publicized miracles." Jess rolled her eyes. "I knew there'd be more to the story. There always is." She wiggled her finger over the touchpad of her laptop to wake it up. "My door's always open, you know. Don't be a stranger."

"I won't," said Jess, and then she grabbed her backpack and made the short walk from the principal's office to the college counselor's small room.

She'd dreaded the start of these college meetings, and the only thing that made her consider the possibility of them being tolerable was the fact that Mr. Foster, her seventh grade science teacher, had managed to "escape the gaping and insatiable hellhole of junior high," (his words, of course) and was now Mooremont's college counselor.

She tapped at the ajar door to his office and peeked in. He looked up from his desk. "Come on in." As she did so he added, "Jessica, so nice to see you."

She paused for a moment, foot in the air. He sounded … not entirely unhappy. "Really?" she asked, continuing her progress into the office.

"Of course. You were a good student. I suspect getting you into college is going to be almost no work at all … considering."

"Considering my grades, or considering I'm the

daughter of God?" She set her backpack down and sat in the wooden chair at his desk.

He swallowed hard. "Both, I guess."

She relaxed, hoping he might too. The poor guy was still tightly wound. "Mrs. Thomas says hi."

"Oh. Um. Okay."

"I was just chatting with her."

His head tilted back then nodded slowly, like some deep meaning was dawning on him. "Ah. I see."

"You seem stressed, Mr. Foster."

He exhaled sharply. "Yeah. I really can't complain, though. This job is way easier than teaching."

"Does your job security depend on the number of us who get into college?"

He grunted, the weight returning to his shoulders like old times. "Unfortunately, yes. My job is to somehow make sure people like Gary Higgins and Greg "Wake and Bake" Burns decide a four-year degree and crippling student loan debt is the best decision for them."

Jess nodded agreeably and let Mr. Foster's disdain for Greg wash over her, savoring it for as long as she could without it becoming too obvious. "Well, you don't have to worry about me. I'm going somewhere."

Mr. Foster forced a smile. "Right. So, any ideas of what you want to study?"

"Uh … not history?"

"Not history," echoed Mr. Foster dryly. "I guess that's a start. What about, um … medicine?" He squinted his eyes upon saying the last word, as if bracing himself against what he already knew to be a mistake.

So he'd seen the news. Just like everybody else. The riddled corpse had been blurred out to spare viewers, and wasn't that just nice for them. Maybe someday she would just be a viewer of horrible things in Mooretown, rather than a constant eye witness.

The image of the Mexican man's mangled body hadn't taken a night off from her dreams yet, and she'd all but given up trying to pretend his nationality didn't play a strong subconscious part in the fact that he usually started off as a colorful piñata and morphed into a colander-esque corpse as soon as he'd had the candy beaten out of him.

"Not medicine," she replied.

"Yeah. That ... that makes sense."

He turned in his chair, pulled a file from a hanger, and Jessica saw her name written on the tab. He flipped open the folder, set it on his desk, and then shuffled a few pages deep until he pulled out a sheet titled Initial College Questionnaire. "Why don't we just zip on through this Kafkaesque quagmire of paperwork that the school requires, and then we can dive into the stuff that's actually useful."

Jess nodded and he began going line by line, reading the questions aloud. "Are you planning on attending a four-year university?"

"Yes."

"Do your parents have a college savings account set up for you?"

Jessica laughed.

Mr. Foster glanced up at her, arching an eyebrow.

"Sorry," she said. "Uh, no, I don't see that being a thing."

He nodded and ticked the *No* box.

"Highest level of education for your mother?"

"Uh, I don't think she finished high school."

He ticked the *Some High School* box.

"Highest level of education for your fa—uh." He chanced a look up at her, and she frowned.

"I don't think He went to school. But He knows a lot of stuff anyway."

Mr. Foster nodded. "There's not an *All Knowing* box …"

She waved him off. "Oh no, He's not all knowing. He's just knowing and all that. Bad translation."

The counselor's eyes narrowed at her. Clearly he thought she was screwing with him. "How about I just check *Unknown*?"

"Yeah, that works."

By the time they'd made it through the entire form, Jess was thoroughly discouraged about her financial outlook and Mr. Foster was clearly on the verge of a serious existential crisis.

"So you're *not* interested in a religious university?" he asked for the second time.

"No, why would I be?"

He cackled, one eye wide, and threw his hands into the air. "Ha! Why would she be?" he asked no one.

The bell echoed in from the hallway, and she thought it best if she left in a hurry. Mr. Foster clearly needed time to regroup. "See you next week," she said and then rushed out of his office.

Before heading to the cafeteria, she peeked in on Mrs. Thomas, who was busy typing away on her laptop. "Hey, would you maybe check in with Mr. Foster whenever you have a break? He's a little on edge."

Mrs. Thomas beamed as if she actually knew what Jess was talking about. "Of course."

Jessica breathed deep, wondered briefly if she could win enough scratch-offs to pay for her education without anyone growing too suspicious, and then headed to the parking lot to catch up with Chris and Miranda for lunch.

* * *

Chris and Miranda seemed to find the story of Jess's first college counseling session highly amusing, so there was that, at least.

As seniors, they were allowed to eat off-campus, which meant that lunch had become a glorious succession of Gordon's burgers as often as they could afford it, which, thanks to the last bit of the child support money Chris's wealthy father owed, turned out to be more days than not, Chris's treat.

The heat of the August sun was stifling, and Jess didn't have much of an appetite, so she'd opted for a single rather than a double today. The three of them had just gotten their food and found an open booth when she heard her name shouted from the front door.

"Hey, McCloud! I got something to say to you."

"I could never hear his voice again and live a happy

life," she grumbled to Miranda before turning toward the source of the voice.

Trent, Courtney, Sandra, and Drew stood in the entryway of the restaurant, with Trent and Courtney in the lead. The twins stomped over, and Jess prepared herself for whatever heap of bullshit they were about to pile on.

"Don't worry," Chris mumbled, "I'll handle him."

"Don't," Jess replied. "It's too hot to fight. Just let them get it out of their system and then hopefully they'll go away."

The restaurant was packed with seniors, and Jessica found that her anxiety over what accusations might be hurled her way in front of her peers went up like flash paper, burning for only an instant until—poof!—it was gone. What in her Father's name could Trent possibly say about her that hadn't already been said a thousand times? If anything, he would just come off as a broken record, which certainly didn't reflect poorly on *her*.

Am I becoming immune to insults? It was a nice idea. Without being aware of it, she let a smile turn the corners of her mouth just as Trent paused at the end of the table, his feet planted shoulder width apart, fists braced on his hips.

"What are you smiling about, McCloud?"

Dewy sweat droplets glistened at the ends of his scrappy attempt at a mustache, and she had a hard time taking her eyes off of it.

I wonder if he's ever even kissed a girl.
DOES HIS SISTER COUNT?
What?!

"McCloud! I'm talking to you!"

"Huh?"

"I said, what are you smiling about? You think this is all some joke?"

Jess didn't have to look around to know the other restaurant goers had paused in their meal to watch the scene unfold. It was what she would do, if this sort of thing ever happened to anyone else, which it never seemed to.

But she'd been here before, embroiled in a situation that was focused solely on her humiliation. Only, this time she wasn't in the mood to be humiliated. Maybe she'd simply met her limit of horror for the year.

"Think *what* is all some joke?" she asked.

"Uh, our lives," said Courtney as she stepped forward to stand next to her brother. "You're trying to ruin our lives because we're holy."

"I guess I'm confused," Jess began. "Or maybe we have different understandings of what the word 'holy' means. For me, it's not synonymous with 'annoying.'" She pressed her lips together, pouting apologetically.

But Trent must have already rehearsed in his mind how this would go, because he ignored her comment and kept forging on. "If you think I'm too afraid to call you out—"

"I never thought that."

"Then you're wrong! I'm not scared of you, no matter *what* people say you can do." He shot a quick pointed look at Chris before turning back to her. "You're trying to tear our family apart, aren't you? You're jealous of us because our parents are married, unlike *these* two you hang out with." He nodded at Miranda and Chris. "So you decided to stick your big, probably Jewish, Antichrist nose into my parents' marriage to tear us apart."

Jessica laughed without meaning to. Of all the things she'd been accused of being, Jewish was definitely the best. Jews *were* the chosen people, after all. But more importantly, *this* was what he was going on about? He was mad at her for both of his parents cheating on each other for years?

Before she could point that out, Miranda did it for her. "Are you seriously blaming Jessica for your parents fucking around on each other?"

"What my parents do is their business, not yours!" Trent said.

Courtney's accusatory tone was stymied by her confusion as she spat, "So now you're trying to slander our father, too?"

The corner of Miranda's upper lip cinched in confusion and she glanced at Jessica, who shrugged. Maybe Courtney didn't know about that half of the equation.

Courtney looked at her brother for backup and quickly realized, as he avoided her gaze, that she wouldn't get any. "Our dad didn't cheat, Trent." Perhaps it was supposed to be a correction, but it sounded closer to a question. "It was just our unfaithful Jezebel mother."

Trent set his jaw, then mumbled toward his shoulder, "No. It was dad, too."

Jessica laughed, and this time it was very much on purpose. This was too sweet. "You didn't know?" A sour joy rushed through her. "Your dad's been cheating for at least"—she did the math—"twelve years."

TWENTY-TWO.

Courtney's head jerked around toward her brother, her eyes shooting daggers. "How long have you known?" she demanded softly.

"A while," he said nonchalantly. "But it doesn't matter. He's a man. If he cheated, it's because our mom wasn't doing her wifely duties and he had no choice." Courtney didn't seem convinced, but Trent had regained his righteous momentum, and there seemed to be no stopping him now. "It's no wonder she won't stop talking about you at dinner. A slut like her would naturally be drawn to the daughter of Mooretown's biggest slut."

Chris jumped up from the booth, his chest bumping Trent's and sending the Wurst son back a step to keep his footing. Chris stared down at him. "You shouldn't talk about your sister that way."

"Huh?"

It wasn't quite a hit as far as insults go, but Jess sort of scrapped together the logic of it and appreciated the sentiment.

"Lunchtime's over," Chris repeated. "You have three seconds to get out of my sight before I tell everyone what I caught you doing behind the equipment shed last year."

Trent stepped back immediately.

"What's he talking about?" Courtney asked.

Trent grabbed her by the wrist. "Doesn't matter. Come on."

Courtney sneered at him and jerked her arm free of his grasp, but as he stormed from Gordon's, she followed him out all the same.

Chris sat back down at the booth, and Jess grinned at him. "You didn't have to."

He nodded. "I know. But I wanted to."

Miranda sipped the last of her Dr. Pepper through the straw. "What'd you catch him doing behind the equipment shed?"

Chris shook his head. "Trust me, you don't want to know."

Jessica somehow *knew* what was about to happen before His voice ever filled her skull:

HE WAS CALLING YOUR NAME WHILE HE SPILLED HIS SEED.

The image of it flashed in her mind and she spit out her partially chewed fry, sending mushed potato bits across the table and onto Miranda's tray. "Jesus fucking Christ …"

Chris frowned sympathetically. "He told you, didn't He?"

Jess felt like she was going to be sick. "And showed me."

Chris gagged. "That's unfortunate."

"Do I want to know?" Miranda asked hesitantly.

Jess shook her head quickly then pushed her food away from her when the salty smell of it started to churn her stomach. "That whole family is the worst."

* * *

"Chris, stop the car."

Jessica braced a palm on the dashboard as he came to a

sudden stop just before the green light at the main intersection of Mooretown.

"Are you kidding me?" she muttered, staring at the object out the window. She opened the passenger-side door of the truck and climbed down just as Chris asked her what was wrong.

She jogged the four steps to the light pole and ripped off the flyer that was glued to it, giving it a close reading. Yep. It was as bad as she thought.

She jumped back in the truck, the paper still clutched in her fist.

"What is it?" Chris asked again. "You scared the shit out of me."

She held it up for him to see, and he slowly read it, moving his lips as he did so, until he finally finished with, "Well damn."

"I should've expected something like this, with Mrs. Wurst being so silent lately."

"Maybe it's not as bad as it seems. I mean, there are probably plenty of people who would love for someone to start a church devoted to them."

Jess's mouth hung open as she stared at him incredulously. "Yeah. Psychopaths. No one in their right mind wants to be worshiped with their very own church."

A car honked behind them, and Chris pulled forward through the light, which had already cycled back through to green.

"What about Jesus?" he asked. "He wanted a church to worship him."

"I don't know that it was his end game to have a bunch

of people collecting money in his name and twisting his words," she said bitterly. "Plus, have you met Jesus?"

It was a rhetorical question. Of course he hadn't met Jesus. Most people hadn't.

But he said, "Sort of. I mean, I let him into my heart when I was like eight."

That was a new one. "You let him into your heart?"

Chris shrugged. "Yeah." He glanced thoughtfully at her. "I forget you don't know anything about all this. It's what people do at church and youth group. You say, 'Jesus, I invite you into my heart. Get in there, please.' And then Jesus enters your heart."

"I think you might be confusing him with Dracula," she said.

"He was in my dream a few months ago."

"Dracula?"

"No, Jesus. It was weird."

"Tell me about it. He likes to poke his head into mine, too." She stared out the window, wondering what it would be like to have a real sex dream without her half-brother showing up. She closed her eyes and tried for the first time to conjure a real sexual fantasy. Maybe if she were awake and built the dream herself, Jesus wouldn't be able to interlope.

"This was different, though," Chris said, uncertainty in his voice.

"How so?" It should have been easy to concoct a fantasy with her and Chris in the truck when she was already with Chris in the truck, but maybe the two scenarios were too close for it to work, and her fantasy even included Mrs. Wurst's shoddy flyer for First Girl Christ Church.

"Well, you and me were ... making out in my truck—"

"Mm-hmm?" She let him paint the picture for her.

"And then you took your shirt off, and I was able to undo your bra super quick, which is weird, because I'm not even sure how bras are fastened—"

"Mm-hmm?" It was easy enough to imagine, since it followed along so closely with the narrative of her last sex dream.

"And then Jesus showed up and started talking to you about your miracle."

Shit. The picture he was painting with broad strokes was not just similar but *identical* to the last sex dream she's had. "Hold on. What?" She opened her eyes.

"Yeah, I'm telling you, it was weird." He laughed. "It was sort of like that one dream you had a while back with Jameson Fractal when Jesus showed up in Germany. So like, you were there and Jesus was talking with you about ... God. And then I thanked him, but he didn't seem too big on it ..."

"Uh ..."

"I know. Crazy."

"Yes, but not for the reason you're thinking."

He glanced at her. "What do you mean?"

"What night was this, Chris?"

He was still considering it as they pulled into her driveway. "I guess it was that same night of the wreck, actually. Yeah, that was it. I woke up, and then couldn't go back to sleep because I was anxious and because we have this

It's a Miracle!

woodpecker in our back yard that acts like it's on meth, so I came over to your place."

It was just too much of a coincidence. But she didn't know what to make of it.

"What's so crazy about it?" he asked. "Besides the obvious."

She sucked in a lungful of air then for some reason she wasn't quite sure of yet, decided against explaining her theory. "Nothing. Never mind. I had a dream about Jesus last night is all." She smiled at him, leaned in for a kiss, then opened the truck door, sliding out of the seat and grabbing her backpack as she went. "See you tomorrow."

"Don't forget first after-school practice of the season."

"Yep. Got it." She pushed the door closed, waved goodbye, and the headed inside.

So Chris had the same dream as her. That was clear enough.

But how? Why?

Chapter Nine

The Mexicans' first pre-season game should have come and gone unnoticed. It was just a pre-season game, who cared? Pre-season results didn't matter and first string almost never played a minute, so really it wasn't more than a scrimmage. And in the years prior to Jessica's success as the Mexicans' star kicker, pre-season had slipped in quietly then pulled the old Irish good-bye without any recognizable spark of excitement. While some things had change since she'd joined the team, one thing was still a guarantee: pre-season games held no intrinsic entertainment, except to the few fans who liked to see one team unequivocally trounce the other, which everyone knew would be the case when Mooremont played Van Dyke, a science and technology magnet school with hardly enough men to put together a first-string offense and defense.

In the days leading up to that showdown, Jessica doubted whether she would even get a chance to play, instead allowing the back-up kicker have his time to shine before he spent the season warming the bench and trying not to brood *too* hard about being second-string to a girl. But apparently the small chance that something *might* happen that would require Jessica to take the field was enough to attract a dozen news vans to the Mooremont parking lot early Friday morning, where they double- and triple-parked across the prime spaces outside the stadium, waiting out the heat until it was closer to game time and they had no choice but to crawl out of the air conditioned vehicles and set up.

After dropping off her equipment in the locker rooms to the side of the field, Jessica met up with Chris, who'd just done the same, and they crossed in front of the stands and past the vans on their way back to the glorious air conditioning of the school, where they'd wait and hydrate until the last possible moment.

The Channel Six news van was, of course, among the throng. And as they passed by it, Jessica spied Eugene Thornton grazing on a Gordon's burger in the front seat, his feet up on the dash and so engrossed in his food that he didn't notice who had stopped to stare.

"Man I hate that guy," she said.

Chris paused and followed her gaze. "How's he just gonna eat a Gordon's burger like that?"

Jess understood. Eugene didn't deserve a Gordon's burger.

When the reporter happened to glance up—perhaps because he could sense two teenagers were staring him down from only fifteen feet away—his eyes popped open at the discovery of who he was face to face with.

"You see any cameras rolling?" Chris asked out of the corner of his mouth.

"Nope."

He grabbed her and pulled her toward him, pressing his lips down on hers, putting on a real show. She cracked open an eye to get a look at Eugene, whose mouth gaped open, exposing his partially masticated food. Then he began bark orders to whoever was in the back of the van. When the frantic reporter turned his attention to the amorous scene again, Chris broke the kiss. Then he turned toward Eugene, a big grin on the his face, and slowly lifted both middle fingers into the air before motioning with a nod for Jess to keep walking.

She laughed and they trotted off before Eugene Thornton could capture even half a second of the moment on camera.

Small victories, she thought. *You have to take the small ones, especially when you never get the big ones.*

As they entered into the heavenly chill of the main building, Jess split off from her boyfriend to hit the ladies' room down the hall, telling him she'd meet up with him in Coach Rex's office.

She was just about to stroll into the ladies' restroom when someone came out of the men's room on the other side of the hall dressed head to toe in white, and immediate warning alarms blared in her skull, causing her to pause until her brain could catch up.

Once it did, she took a step back and the man didn't seem to notice her until she pointedly spat, "Who let *you* in?"

Jimmy Dean looked up and emitted a surprised "Ay!" before composing himself. "Jessica. How are you?"

"Screw you, Jimmy. I know you're just here to protest me."

He nodded sadly. "Is that what you think?"

Was that a joke? She laughed, because clearly it was a joke. "Yes, that's exactly what I think. You enjoy ruining my life."

He tsk-ed and shook his head slowly. "No, Jessica. That's not it. It's actually the opposite." He stepped closer, and as much as she wanted to back away from him, she stood her ground. "You remember our ice cream dates?"

"Yes," she said begrudgingly. She folded her arms across her chest.

"Remember when I said I thought of you as a daughter?"

She didn't bother replying, because what she wanted to say would've been too mean.

"I meant it," he said. "Truly. I did. And do."

What was she supposed to do with someone like Jimmy? The only person she knew who'd ever been able to adequately handle his bullshit was her mother, so she took a page from Destinee's playbook. "Then what the fuck, Jimmy?"

His eyebrows shot up for a millisecond at her response. "You're more and more like your mother every day."

She rolled her eyes before realizing that was *also* a very Destinee response.

"I can see how you would misinterpret my actions," he said. "The media do an impressive job of weaving their own narratives, and I haven't been great about keeping you in the loop. For that I apologize."

Ugh. She hated how intrigued he was making her. "You're full of it, Jimmy." It didn't exactly make sense anyway, Church Jimmy talking about Ice Cream Jimmy. Did the two of them ever communicate? But she knew without a doubt that she was talking to Church Jimmy, because Ice Cream Jimmy didn't use words like *narrative* and *apologize*.

"Jessica." His voice was watery and pleading. She didn't trust it. But a part of her must not have completely mistrusted it, because she let him continue. "I know it might seem like I'm against you, but I'm not. I'm with you. I've been with you all along. Don't you see? The world would have long since torn you up and spit you out if I hadn't done what I did."

"Yeah, that makes no sense. And I gotta pee, so you better get to the point."

He wiped his hands down his face—a strangely Ice Cream Jimmy thing to do. "No one wants to hear about God's daughter right now. The safest thing you could do would be to pretend you aren't who you are until the world is ready. I'm helping you do that. Time and time again people like me—handsome, charismatic, wise, hard-working, pull-yourself-up-by-the-bootstraps, salt-of-the-earth white men—have been able to easily earn their way into high ranking positions in society, so that's what I'm doing. I'm climbing the ladder so that I can pull you up with me without anyone noticing."

"Yeah, you're doing a great job with that last part, the no one noticing part. You're doing such a great job that *I* didn't even notice." She pressed her lips together and arched an eyebrow at him impatiently.

"We need each other," he said flatly, his soft, nurturing tone kicked to the curb by stark assuredness. "You don't have to accept it, but it's a reality. My poll numbers have been abysmal since Ruth Wurst betrayed me like a cold-hearted Judas, and if I don't win this election, I'm done. Which means we're *both* done. I can't pave the way for you if I lose. And then what? The world will miss out on your message."

Is he bullshitting me?

I … BELIEVE SO.

But you're not sure?

I LEARNED MY LESSON LONG AGO ABOUT READING JIMMY'S THOUGHTS. THE LORD DAREST NOT TREAD THERE ANYMORE. IT IS A DARK PLACE.

He's actually making a little bit of sense, though.

RIGHT?

"Whatever, Jimmy, I have to pee."

"Think about what I said, Jessica. The world needs you, and you need me. Don't be shortsighted on this."

She waved him off and headed into the bathroom (another place where the Lord had learned the hard way that He darest not tread), grateful for a moment of solitude to consider her options. But all she could think was, God dammit, Jimmy.

* * *

By the time Jessica and Chris walked into the McCloud

home that night, carrying two plastic bags full of Pacos Tacos, Coach Rex was already on his second post-game beer, and Destinee was donning her after-work leopard-print sweat pants.

As Jess had suspected, she hadn't been asked even once to take the field during the pre-season game against Van Dyke—unfortunately leaving her with too much time on her hands to recap her conversation with Jimmy Dean again and again—but she was starving nonetheless.

They plopped the bags onto the center of the kitchen table, and everyone gathered around, sorting through for their order. Chris stacked five crispy tacos in front of himself, and Jess assumed his lack of playing time was to blame for his diminished appetite.

"Almost felt sorry for the Dykes," Destinee said through a mouthful of burrito.

"I don't think that's their mascot, Mom."

Destinee shrugged. "Maybe not. A buncha dykes woulda put up a better fight, though. It was like everyone on the other team was anemic, the way they were huffin' and puffin'. Thought you were gonna have to resurrect a few of them on the field, baby." She swigged her beer.

"You talk to Jimmy?" Jess asked her mother. She tried to sound offhand, but as soon as the words had left her mouth, she understood that there was no way to bring up Jimmy Dean around the McCloud household in an offhanded way.

"The hell would I do that for?"

Jess shrugged. "Just wondering. I mean, he was there, you were there. It could happen." She glanced up from her food to find both Chris and Destinee staring at her like hawks. (Coach Rex continued doing X-Rated things to his taco, oblivious to what everyone else was picking up on.)

"What'd he say to you?" Destinee asked.

"I mean, you know Jimmy. It was nonsense. He said"—*we need each other*—"some bull about all that he's done being for my sake."

Destinee threw her head back. "Ha! Right." She laughed until she had to wipe away a tear. "Man. Jimmy just doesn't stop, huh? So is that why he was holding that *Repent sinners! Denounce the Antichrist!* sign behind the end zone tonight? Was that for your sake, too?"

Jess chuckled along with everyone else, but somehow her mother's certainty only made Jessica less certain that he was lying. Jimmy's claim seemed so far off from his actions that surely he couldn't expect her to believe any of it unless there actually was some truth to it. No one would lie that blatantly, right?

Her mind traveled back a handful of hours to when she passed Jimmy and the other White Light Church protestors on her way from the school to the locker rooms, just before game time. He'd made eye contact and given her a simple nod, like they were in cahoots with one another, like it was all one big game and they were playing for the same team. Maybe he actually believed what he'd said, whether it was reality or not.

Certainly media could be biased and make up stories out of nowhere—she knew that much from personal experience. Was Jimmy just as much of a victim as Jessica in all of it?

She crunched into a taco and allowed herself a moment of savory goodness while the dust settled around the thought so she could examine it more closely.

Mmm ... cheese and beef and onions and shredded lettuce ...

A thin layer of grease coating the walls of her stomach provided the necessary comfort for her to begin thinking more clearly, and she decided that regardless of whether Jimmy was being honest, the way he'd martyred her and Destinee on the stage in front of all those people at White Light Church would never be okay or excusable. Even the momentary memory of it was enough for her to decide that she was willing to do whatever she could to make sure Jimmy didn't get elected.

Maybe he could do what he said, maybe he could start as mayor and climb the ladder, pulling her up behind him, but when it came down to it, she didn't want to follow Jimmy anywhere, not even up a ladder to power, especially not if he was always a rung or two above her. And she simply wouldn't be able to stomach the sight of his awful, handsome Church Jimmy smile if he won.

"And it's only going to get worse," Chris said as Jessica clued back into the conversation.

"What's only going to get worse?"

"The craziness at the games."

"Oh. Yeah, that was pretty bad today," she conceded. It hadn't bothered her so much because she didn't have to play and was able to hang out on the sidelines with her back to it all.

"I think you're right, Chris. It'll only get worse," Coach

Rex said. Destinee's body twitched slightly and Rex jumped in his chair and sucked in air as he shot a glance at Destinee, then seemed to understand what the kick was about. He turned to Jessica. "Not your fault, though. You just be you."

Jessica sighed and felt her shoulders grow heavy. Of course it was her fault. There had been an entire decade where no one gave two shits about the Mooremont Mexicans before she joined the team. Was it worth winning championships to put her teammates, who'd stood by her side for the past two years, through the worst media circus yet?

Maybe it was just her tiredness from the late night, or her confusion after her conversation with Jimmy, or the fallout of the grease bomb she'd just ingested, or the fact that there was a lightning storm in the forecast for the next couple days (whether meteorologists realized it yet or not), but a new realization seemed to settle in her chest, one she knew better than to share with any of the well-meaning people who sat around the kitchen table at the McCloud home: *I need to quit the football team.*

Chapter Ten

Jessica was on a mission. It felt good. She had a clear goal. She had a purpose. Adults always talked about discovering a sense of purpose, and while she'd been born into a fairly obvious one, she'd assumed that wasn't what adults meant. They meant something simpler, something less likely to get a person tortured and nailed to a cross.

She was three minutes early for her meeting, but she didn't care.

Her sudden arrival as she let herself into Mr. Foster's office caught him with ramen noodles dangling from his mouth. They flapped around as he yanked his head up, sending small flicks of broth onto his wrinkled sea-foam button-up.

As he tried to corral the noodles into his mouth with his chopsticks, Jessica started in on him with her big news. "Politics. I want to study politics."

He choked for a second, but was able to recover enough to croak, "Why in God's name … ?"

"I want to learn all about politics so I can destroy someone."

Mr. Foster scooted the Styrofoam cup to the side of his desk and leaned back in his chair, nodding his understanding. "That's why most people get into it, I suppose."

"So where do I start? The sooner the better."

He took his time evaluating her, inspecting her expression intently. "Well, considering how much people seem to enjoy blending government and religion nowadays, you might just be a shoo-in for basically any school's political science department ..."

She waited silently but impatiently for him to get through his obligatory opining. She knew he needed to mull things over before he could get on board. And for some reason, she really wanted him on board. She needed the Mr. Foster seal of approval.

"But I guess it wouldn't hurt for you to start getting involved in local politics this year. Have a little something to put on your resume."

That's what she'd hoped he'd say. "Perfect. How do I get started with that?"

He eyed her skeptically. "This wouldn't happen to have anything to do with the ritual bloodbath of a mayor's race over in Midland, would it?"

"Why does that matter?"

"Motives are everything, Jess."

She sighed and decided she should probably sit down and stop hovering over him. "I just don't want to see him win."

"Neither do I," said Mr. Foster quickly, surprising her.

"Why do *you* hate Jimmy?"

"Hate is a strong word," he hedged, "but it's not quite strong enough. Disdain is closer, loathing is more like it."

Jessica cackled. Hearing someone bash Jimmy was always a treat. "But why?"

He shrugged. "What's there to like about him? He's the worst of religion and he's trying to converge with the worst of politics. He's a monster. Someone should stop him."

"So that's what I want to do." Surely he had to understand that.

He hesitated and steepled his fingers together in front of his mouth. "Right. But I'm not sure you're the best person to take him down."

"And why's that?" she asked crossly.

"Because, Jess, you're a *nice* person. Even if you do want to destroy him—which, by the way, you probably shouldn't go around telling people that you want to 'destroy' others —your motive stems from a selfless love for others and a desire to protect them. Because you're nice. Politics is the playground of personality disorders. If you're not a narcissist, sociopath, or psychopath, you're just chum in the water for narcissists, sociopaths, and psychopaths."

"I don't know what that means." Why wouldn't he just agree to help her?

He sighed. "It means I would hate to see you get into politics. But if that's what you want to study, far be it from me to stop you. And as ill-advised as it seems to be for you to dip your toes into the murky, polluted waters of politics before you're even old enough to vote, it's always a good idea to try out the field before you commit to studying it for four years. Maybe you can get it out of your system now and then spare yourself some pain and suffering by finding a less dangerous, exhausting, and soul-sucking career. Like working in a mental hospital. Or a maximum-security prison. Or a public school."

He dragged a napkin over his desk, mopping up droplets of spilled broth, and then pulled over his laptop, from where it tottered precariously at the edge of his desk, to rest in front of him. As he began typing quickly, he said, "Okay. So do you want to stay in state or go out of state?"

She may not get his outright seal of approval, but at least he was on board, even if he clearly thought it was a terrible idea. "Which one did you say *didn't* cost an arm and a leg?"

His head leaned from side to side. "Eh … They both do. But in-state only requires your non-dominant arm."

* * *

It felt unmistakably scummy to use resurrection as a photo op, but Wendy Peterman insisted that if Jessica wanted to get into politics, she needed to get used to scummy, maybe even going so far as to embrace it.

After two months away from Midland Memorial Hospital, Jessica had assumed it would be strange walking back through the sliding glass doors and into her private room in the near-empty wing. But the room was just as she'd left it on her birthday, and it felt like almost no time had passed. The orderlies that hadn't graduated after the summer smiled at her, and the doctors said hello like she'd never left. And there was no resentment there. She'd expected resentment. After all, she'd left them in the lurch to shoulder the responsibility of keeping people alive without the safety net of her miracle. The guilt had definitely eaten at her during her time away, and her only defense against it was that the few hundred deaths she could have prevented over that period of time was a drop in the bucket on a worldwide scale. Especially when considering Asia. It'd occurred to her once she'd returned that maybe the doctors and nurses had come to the same conclusion. Or maybe they'd heard about her birthday. (What was she thinking? Of course they'd heard.) Maybe after the debacle with the young man—who she'd later found out was a hitman for the Zeta cartel out of Nuevo Laredo and had spent nearly a week in the Rio Grande before being discovered—the good people at Midland Memorial understood why she would need a break from performing her miracle. If anyone understood the burden of having people's lives in your hands, it was these folks.

She jerked her hands back from the body as the girl's eyes shot open. "Whoa." Jess took a quick step back. Spacing out while resurrecting wasn't a great idea, and she had a feeling it hadn't made for a very good photo. She glanced over at the photographer, who frowned at the view screen of his camera.

"Eh … can I just have you stand next to the body—er—patient? Be sure to smile."

Jess moved closer to the girl, whose chest heaved up and down as she tried to reacquaint herself with the harsh reality of being yanked away from the afterlife. She gazed up at Jessica. "Who're you?"

"Uhh ..."

The girl was about Jessica's age, plus or minus two years.

"Can you get her to sitting?" the photographer asked. "Maybe put your arm around her?"

"Who're you?" the girl asked again.

"Jessica," said Jessica.

"Oh hey! That's my name, too!"

Jessica had never felt a particular desire to get to know the people she brought back. Whoever the hospital brought her, she fixed and then sent on their merry way. Sharing a name with this one didn't sit well with her, and Jess tried not to look at the two vampiric pinholes in the other Jessica's neck where the rattler had nipped her at a family picnic. The holes would close eventually, and not even a scar would remain.

"What happened?" asked Snake Bite Jessica, as the assigned nurse helped her sit up slowly.

"A little closer together," instructed the photographer, waving his hand until Christ Child Jessica's right hip was up against Snake Bite Jessica's left hip.

"Smile!" he demanded, like that was the obvious thing to do in this situation.

Both Jessicas smiled as instructed, and once that was done, Christ Child Jessica asked the nurse if that was the last patient of the afternoon. When the nurse nodded, Christ Child Jessica fled the room. She hated the awkward post-resurrection conversations between the nurses and miracle patients, which sometimes turned into shouting matches, sometimes involved more crying than Jessica would ever be comfortable with, but mostly involved the nurse tediously repeating everything.

She made her way straight to the closest bathroom to splash water on her face and reapply some makeup before her endorsement speech.

After pulling her straight brown hair back with the hair tie she kept around her wrist, she cupped her hands underneath the running faucet and ladled the water onto her face. She hadn't meant to moan, but she did.

A flush in one of the stalls snapped her out of her indulgence, and she looked up to see Dr. Fractal appear in the mirror before walking up to the next sink over.

"Jessica! So nice to see you here again."

"Good to be here," she lied.

"Are you resuming your internship?"

Jess shook her head. "No, just here today."

The woman narrowed her eyes thoughtfully. "Hmm ... Is it a coincidence that you're here the same day they're building a red, white, and blue stage in the parking lot for Polly Cox?"

How'd she put that together so quickly? Well, I guess she's a doctor, so ...

"No coincidence. I'm endorsing her today."

Dr. Fractal bit back a smile. "Ah. Okay. I'm sure your support will go a long way."

"I really just don't want to see Jimmy win."

Dr. Fractal nodded solemnly. "I get that. No sane person wants to see him win. But, you know, Polly Cox hasn't been a particularly straightforward or honest politician herself. And is getting involved in politics really the best idea for you? Are you even old enough to vote?"

Dr. Fractal proceeded to scrub her hands thoroughly.

"Well, no, but if I *could,* and I lived in Midland, I would vote for Mayor Cox."

The doctor toweled off and then turned to Jessica. "Listen. I'm going to tell you what I told my brother. It's one thing to go vote your conscience, but it's another to step forward and publicly endorse a candidate. And trust me, when I vote in March, I'll be voting for Polly Cox, even if she *is* involved in some shady stuff, but there's a difference between giving someone your vote and endorsing them. In the end, a politician is a politician, which means they're not your friend."

Jessica nodded. This sounded awfully similar to what Mr. Foster had told her. "Thanks. But I think I'll be all right." Did she appreciate the advice? Sure. But having adults tell her she didn't know what she was getting into was starting to grate on her.

Dr. Fractal sighed heavily but smiled. "Yeah, that's what my brother said too."

"Wait. Which brother?"

"My only brother. Jameson."

Jess tried to play it cool. "Oh yeah? Who'd he endorse?"

"Well, nobody yet, but Polly Cox." She paused and

cocked her head slightly to the side. "Did you not hear that he's also doing that today?"

"No ..." Jess said slowly, feeling a secret hope build inside her. "Is he doing that up in Vancouver, or ...?"

"No, no. Filming there wrapped last month. Wait, did you not see him outside?"

"Outside?" she echoed moronically.

Dr. Fractal nodded. "Yeah, he's been hanging out in my office all day. He said he was slated to give his endorsement right after yours."

She felt her breakfast try to leap free of the confines of her stomach. "He knows who I am?"

Dr. Fractal laughed. "Ah I see. Another fan. Figures. Yes, Jessica, he knows who you are. Most people in this state do by now. You're kind of a celebrity."

That word. What was it about that word that felt like a punch to the throat? It didn't even have the qualifier "local" before it.

Jessica was a celebrity.

She was a celebrity who was about to meet another celebrity.

She was a celebrity who was about to meet the sexiest celebrity on the planet.

"Well," said Dr. Fractal casually, like she hadn't just dropped a dirty bomb on Jessica's emotions, "for what it's worth, I genuinely wish both of you only the best in your brush with politics. Maybe it'll—"

Whatever she said after that was lost to Jessica's mind, which had officially short circuited. "Yeah, thanks," she murmured as the doctor left the restroom.

Jess thought it best to hole up in the bathroom for a little longer, on the off chance that her roiling stomach decide to lose a few pounds of water weight all at once. Why was she so terrified? She repeated the new reality over and over to herself in an attempt to desensitize.

I'm going to meet Jameson Fractal today.

Chapter Eleven

The plastic banners, some blue with white stars, some red with white stripes, billowed in the gusty, tepid late-summer wind. Media scurried around to set up, and perhaps because they were promised a good sound bite or ten from her later, they didn't bother Jessica for the time being.

She stood with her arms crossed, mind entirely unfocused as Wendy continued to grill her on her speech, which she'd spent the night before obsessively committing to memory so she didn't botch things as badly as she did the last time she spoke in front of this many cameras.

Destinee approached and stood between her daughter and the PR specialist. "Hey, baby—sorry to interrupt—I got you a bottle of water."

Jess took it from her and gulped it down. How had her mouth gotten so dry? She kept chugging until it occurred to her that she might be overtaken by a sudden urge to pee

It's a Miracle!

while she was onstage. She stopped drinking immediately and screwed back on the top. "Thanks."

"Start over from the beginning with those note cards," Wendy suggested. "Three more times, and you'll be golden."

Easy enough. Wendy had written the endorsement speech for Jessica, so it flowed well and in no way implied Jessica was amassing an army of undead. The PR specialist had even spent time coaching Jess over the phone about which words to stress more than others. All she needed now was for the nervousness at meeting Jameson Fractal to stop making her want to projectile vomit on everyone within a five-mile radius.

Outside of the media, the crowd was mostly composed of people in scrubs, who must've either just gotten off their shift for the day or decided to spend their dinner break watching the spectacle. Jessica passed unnoticed behind the audience toward Destinee's car, where there was AC and more quiet to focus, flipping through her note cards, one after the other, as she walked.

"Oh shit. Sorry!" she said, looking up at whoever she'd just run into. Her brain had difficulty processing *that* face in *this* situation. Out of the context of school, Jessica almost didn't recognize Mrs. Thomas.

"Jessica," she said cheerily. "How are you feeling?"

"Uh, fine. Why are you—" and then it became obvious. The congressman. "Oh right. Your husband's introducing me. I guess I forget you're married sometimes."

Mrs. Thomas laughed. "So do I sometimes. Almost never get to see the poor man during election season."

"So is that why you're here?"

Mrs. Thomas adjusted her purse on her shoulder and nodded. "Mostly. I almost never get to see Jack speak, outside of the occasional sound clip. And when he mentioned he'd be introducing you, I figured I could make the short drive if it meant supporting you both. Two birds, one stone, and all that."

Jessica tamped down the mental image of two grackles exploding upon impact with a ricocheting stone. She needed to get a handle on her adrenaline. "Thanks. That means a lot."

Mrs. Thomas leaned close, although she really didn't need to since they were far enough away from the fray that no one could hear their conversation. "You know, I'm proud of you for doing this."

"Huh?" Jessica had naturally assumed that Mrs. Thomas wouldn't support the idea of using her status for political purposes, considering it exploitation, which it was.

"This!" Mrs. Thomas said, waving around at the staging area. "I've always wondered when you would begin to step into the role your Father gave you. I'm glad you finally are."

And now Jessica was flat out confused. This didn't seem to jibe at all with what Mrs. Thomas had said in the past. "Really? I thought … well, it just seems like you've always said I shouldn't limit myself to what God wanted me to do."

"Oh, psh." Mrs. Thomas waved off that idea. "No, I never said anything like that. I've always wanted you to *stop* limiting yourself. And I think that's what you're doing here today, pushing the limits you've set on yourself."

Jessica returned Mrs. Thomas's pleasant smile. "Oh. Okay. Well, thanks."

"I see your mother is here to support you," Mrs. Thomas added, nodding over at Destinee's old Nissan, where her mother and Rex were clearly making out in the front seat. "You're lucky to have such a good mother. I wish my own had been as supportive as she is."

"Yeah," said Jessica, absentmindedly. She'd always assumed Mrs. Thomas *didn't* like Destinee, but perhaps her imagination had simply concocted that out of the fact that Destinee wasn't a huge fan of Mrs. Thomas. It was a relief, though, to know Mrs. Thomas thought favorably of Jessica's only immediate human family.

"I'm glad you have so many adults in your life who are willing to support you in this," Mrs. Thomas added.

Jess's mind flashed back to Mr. Foster's reluctant support, and she hesitated before saying, "Yeah. I guess that's true."

The hesitation didn't slip by unnoticed. "Is there someone who isn't?" Her intense stare forced Jessica to meet her eyes, rather than scan the crowd for the thousandth time.

"Huh? Oh. I mean, Mr. Foster and—"

"Ah." Mrs. Thomas nodded gravely. "I see. Yes. Well, you know, Mr. Foster is … well, I probably shouldn't mention this, but he won't be returning next year. Not that it matters to you, because you'll be gone having the time of your life at college."

"Where's he going?"

Mrs. Thomas shrugged sympathetically. "Not sure." She

sighed. "I understand why he would be opposed to you dipping your toes into politics, considering how poorly he plays the politics at work. I know you like him, and as a person I'm sure he has many redeeming qualities, but"—she leaned closer now—"many in the staff are getting concerned about his sense of entitlement. And just between us, he has a bit of an anger issue." Mrs. Thomas frowned, her shoulders sagging. "It's really disappointing. I stuck my neck out to get him that job, and I really thought he would excel at it, but I guess you just never know with some people."

"Man, that's terrible," said Jess, and she meant it on multiple levels. "Sorry to hear that, Mrs. Thomas. It didn't ... you're not in trouble because of him, are you?"

"Oh no, no. Don't worry about me. I can take care of myself. It's just discouraging when people bite the hand that feeds them.

"Anyway, I didn't mean to get into all that drama. All I wanted to say was that you have plenty of adults who support you, even if a few do not."

Jessica nodded and tried to smile with her eyes, but her mind was a hurricane. She never would've guessed about Mr. Foster, and she wished intensely that she didn't know. Maybe she could've blissfully pretended he was who he seemed to be until she'd left for school. Then it occurred to her what she needed to do.

Is Mr. Foster the Devil?
Inconclusive.
If she'd had to put money on it, she would have gone

the other way and assumed he was an angel, but that was apparently how the Devil worked.

"Um, I better get some more practice in before the speech," she said, excusing herself.

Mrs. Thomas nodded, then her eyes lit up as she remembered. "Oh! Did you hear who's speaking right after you?" She arched a playful brow and Jessica had to laugh.

"Yes, I did."

Mrs. Thomas winked. "Maybe that's also a reason why I'm here, but shh. Don't tell the congressman."

When Wendy found Jessica where she'd decided to wait in Destinee's car with the AC blasting, the sun was dangling only a hair above the horizon. "Show time," Wendy said excitedly, like this wasn't the most petrified Jessica could remember being in her entire life.

Why had politics seemed like a good idea? Perhaps Mr. Foster was the Devil, or a demon at least, but both of those things could have wisdom too, couldn't they? She should have listened to him.

Jess closed the car door behind her and Wendy grabbed Jessica by the shoulders. "Hey. Look at me. This is fine. You're prepared. You're going to do great, and this is going to go a long way toward helping defeat Jimmy Dean in this race."

Jessica nodded determinedly, but Wendy wasn't convinced. "What is it? What's got you so worked up?"

She sighed. There was no way she could explain it all to Wendy, so she decided to pick the least confusing point. "You didn't tell me Jameson Fractal was going to be here."

The only tell of Wendy's poker face was a small twitch at the corner of her mouth. "You're nervous about meeting Jameson?"

"I know it's nothing to you—I mean, you rep him, so you're used to being around him."

Wendy chuckled. "Doesn't mean I don't think he's fine as hell."

"Huh?"

"Jessica. You don't grow immune to looks like Jameson's. I get it, trust me. I'm just glad you're nervous about that and not anything else. If it's any consolation, I've spoken with him, and he's nervous about meeting you, too."

Jessica's jaw dropped, and she struggled against the pull of gravity to close it again. "Why?"

"Because you're God's only begotten daughter," Wendy replied flatly. "Just relax. Once you're done with the endorsement, you just move to the side, and Congressman Thomas will introduce him. He walks on, you shake hands with him, and then, after it's all done, I'll officially introduce you two. Unless you want to meet him beforehand. Would that help?"

"No!" She hadn't meant to shout. "God no. I'll just meet him after."

Wendy nodded. "Okay, whatever you need."

She inhaled deeply, counted to five, and then exhaled. She felt a shade calmer now, or at least she didn't feel the need to vomit on everything.

Jameson Fractal wanted to meet her.

Holy. Shit.

She struggled to focus as Congressman Thomas started in on her introduction.

"Today is a momentous day in Texas history. I'm United States Congressman Thomas, and I've worked my whole adult life to serve the state I love. When my great grandparents came to Texas over a hundred years ago, they brought with them a dream of building something, giving something back. Well, they died penniless. As did my grandparents. But my father took from that an important lesson, that the American dream is one that has to be lucked into, and after dedicating his life to lucking into things, he finally scrapped together a living as the owner of an oil company. And one day before he passed, he said to me, 'Jack, there are two things you should know about life …'"

Jessica leaned over to Wendy. "So is he not the one who's supposed to introduce me, or …?"

"Yeah, he's the one. This is how politicians introduce other people."

"By introducing themselves?"

"Exactly."

"And now," continued Congressman Thomas, "a young lady who needs no introduction. Out of Mooretown, Texas, football sensation and widely proclaimed daughter of God, Jessica McCloud."

The audience applauded. It was a much nicer sound than booing.

Wendy shoved her forward, and she climbed the four stairs up onto the stage, remembering the advice Wendy had given her.

Smile, wave, smile, wave.

She paused at the podium, pulled the note cards from her pocket, and sighed deeply before glancing at the first bullet point to refresh her memory. Then she leaned toward the mic and glanced out into the crowd. Her eyes landed on Mrs. Thomas, who gave her a reassuring smile and two thumbs up.

Maybe I can do this.

"Thank you for coming here today. People told me not to get involved in politics. After all, separation of *church*"—she motioned to herself—"and state." She grinned and the audience knew it was okay to laugh. Her mind went blank. She glanced down at the cards again, found the direction *grin* and then picked it up from there. "But that's actually why I'm here. Because a separation of church and state is necessary for freedom. You should always vote your conscience, what you believe to be right or wrong, but to blur the lines by putting a religious zealot into a position of political power is a completely different animal." She tried not to think about a two-headed giraffe, a mental tic that had developed the night before and only gained steam each time she spoke that line. "Make no mistake. If the Reverend Jimmy Dean is elected as mayor of Midland, he will govern on nothing *but* his religious beliefs, and that will serve the people of White Light Church and White Light Church alone. Don't take communion from a trough? Then Jimmy Dean doesn't care about your freedom.

"But you know who *does* care about your freedom? Mayor Polly Cox. She understands that America is a land of religious freedom, and holds strong Christian faith herself.

But while she might have religious figures of the community who support her, once she's reelected, all of her decisions will be made based upon the constitution of the United States as well as the more relevant one of the Lone Star State. And that's a government for *everyone*, no matter how you take your communion on Sunday." Jess gritted her teeth and forced a smile. The line had been one she'd debated with Wendy more than once, insisting that some voters might not take communion at all, but in the end, Wendy had the winning argument: the candidate with the most Christian votes won. Period. This was Midland, after all, not New York City or San Francisco.

"And that's why I'm here today to officially endorse Mayor Polly Cox. And by securing my endorsement, she's also receiving the seal of approval from someone much, *much* wiser than all of us put together." This was also a line Jessica had argued the validity of with Wendy. "Thank you and I hope that you make the right choice for Midland this March when you reelect Polly Cox as Midland's mayor."

And just like that, it was over. She took a rehearsed step back from the podium to signal to the crowd that she was done, and it felt like a weight lifted from her as the crowd actually applauded.

People were cheering.

For her.

And it wasn't because she'd just performed a miracle.

Granted, making it through the speech without humiliating herself *felt* a little like a miracle, but she knew the difference well by now.

It only gets easier from here, she thought. She took another step back and allowed Congressman Thomas to step forward and introduce the next speaker.

She was pleased to find her nerves had settled now that the brunt of her work was complete. And even when she first laid eyes on the beautiful angel of a man who ascended the stairs, her nerves didn't get the best of her. Then, after a quick scan of her surroundings for Jesus, she determined that this was not in fact a dream; she was about to shake hands with Jameson Fractal.

God, he was tall. And more handsome in real life. How was that possible?

He took his time crossing the stage as he waved and smiled so convincingly that Jess wondered if he didn't actually love this. She wasn't sure how anyone *could*, but Jameson seemed to. *He's an actor, you idiot. Being convincing is his job.*

When his soulful eyes found hers, and his large smile grew even wider (that gesture was genuine, she assured herself—no acting there), it became crystal clear that this was the best day of her life.

He's only eight years older than me. It could happen.

He took his time crossing the stage, owning the space like a powerful god, maybe even an all-powerful one, if such a thing existed. Time seemed to slow down around him as she felt herself pulled under a strange, airy spell.

When he mouthed her name, he used the shorter version like they were old friends—*Jess,* which rhymes with *yes, yes, yes!* He continued toward her, his charming smile in place, his kind eyes squinting happily like maybe this was the best day of *his* life, too. He held out his hand for her, and the natural pull of her body toward his did all the work for her muscles as her hand extended outward. What would happen when her skin brushed his? Would there be a spark of chemistry? Only a few feet separated them now …

The bullet went clear through his temple and out the underside of his jaw.

OH ME DAMN!

The force of it took him to the ground. Jessica grasped helplessly for his hand as he fell and a loud ringing bloomed in her ears.

But even above the ringing she could hear the screams. The volume of them ebbed and flowed with the pulse of her heart beating against her eardrums.

She dropped to her knees and reached down to find *his* pulse, a skill she couldn't believe she had reason to use for the second time in only a handful of months.

He still had one.

That's something.

IF BY SOMETHING YOU MEAN HORRIFYING.

The sight in front of her was so grotesque that it anchored her to the physical world, drawing her focus away from the comments of the Almighty Peanut Gallery.

Jameson's soulful eyes were wide with shock and blood bubbled from his jaw as he struggled to speak during his final breaths.

"Sh …" she said, mostly for her own sake so that she

didn't have to keep seeing that jagged jawbone shard jut out each time his facial muscles contracted.

Someone dropped down by Jessica's side, and when she looked up, she spotted Dr. Fractal. Despite advising both Jessica and Jameson against endorsing a candidate, the woman had shown up to support them.

Strong hands tried to pull Jessica away from Jameson, and she swatted them off.

"God dammit," Dr. Fractal muttered. "No, no, no …"

The doctor applied pressure to the entry and exit points, but outside of that, there wasn't much else to do except stare down at her little brother as he wheezed agonizingly.

YOU KNOW WHAT NEEDS TO BE DONE.

Obviously, but come on! *Jameson? You had to drag him into this part of your plan?*

FIRSTLY, THIS WAS NOT MY PLAN. BUT IT'S NOT LIKE HE'S GOING TO STAY DEAD. SO WHAT'S THE PROBLEM?

What's the problem? I can see his molars. And his mouth is closed!

Enough. God would never understand.

She placed her hands on Dr. Fractal's and gently removed them from Jameson's wounds. "You gotta let him die."

The doctor whipped her head around to look into Jessica's eyes, and she noticed for the first time how similar the siblings looked to one another. Well, pre-bullet.

"Trust me," Jessica said. "You gotta let him die."

Slowly, Dr. Fractal nodded, took a deep breath and

It's a Miracle!

closed her eyes. She clasped her hands together and began praying.

"No no," Jessica said quickly. "Let's not bring Him into this."

"Huh?" The doctor stared helplessly at her.

"The prayer. You don't need it. God doesn't do the miracle thing. I do."

"Oh, okay," she said flatly, and turned her eyes back to her brother.

How much time had passed? It'd felt like an hour, but Jess suspected it was closer to ten seconds. People began trying to get to him now, lots of people.

Through the chaos, Jessica heard her mother's voice. "Back up! Back the fuck up!" Jess glanced up to see Wendy, Destinee, and a few men in suits with ear-pieces clearing out the stage around Jameson's body as Jessica waited patiently for the unfortunate movie star to draw his last breath.

She reached down and there was no pulse.

Ugh. Finally.

She tried to smile reassuringly at Dr. Fractal, but her muscles instead twisted into a grimace that didn't achieve the desired effect. *Screw it*. Jess placed her hands on his chest and felt the pull move through her. He lurched and his wide eyes began darting around again.

Dr. Fractal collapsed on him as the frayed and exposed muscles in his jaw began to weave back together, and Jess took that as her cue to get the hell out of Midland.

Wendy was on the same page. "Okay, he's back," she

said, grabbing Jessica under her armpits and lifting her with surprising strength onto her feet. "Let's get gone."

"I'm sorry," Jess managed to shout to Dr. Fractal before she was dragged away. Whether the doctor heard her or not, Jess couldn't be sure, but she needed to apologize all the same.

Because on a core level—call it women's intuition or divine knowledge—Jessica knew it was all her fault.

Chapter Twelve

"So maybe not political science," Jessica said as she dragged herself into Mr. Foster's office first thing Monday morning. Her conversation with Mrs. Thomas about Mr. Foster's impending departure from Mooremont at the end of the school year had been relegated to the back of her mind by the trauma that had followed it, but that didn't mean it hadn't been bugging her all weekend.

It had taken a backseat, though, to the obvious career decision she'd reached sometime between when she'd resurrected her celebrity crush and when she'd shouted at Destinee to pull over the car twenty miles outside of Midland and spent a solid ten minutes violently blowing chunks into scrub brush along the highway.

The college counselor cracked an eye open from where he sat in his stuffed rolling chair with headphones on. As soon as he spotted her, he yanked off the headphones and straightened his posture. "Jessica! How are you?"

Ugh. He seemed so nice, but her admiration for him felt

dirty and tainted now. She pushed through it. "What are you doing?"

"Huh?"

"What are you doing?"

"Oh this?" He lifted the headphones with a finger. "Just my morning routine of listening to soothing nature sounds and reciting affirmations so the state mandated conformity of this place doesn't make me want to kill myself before lunch."

She *supposed* that was anger, but she couldn't imagine him aiming it at anyone else. Mr. Foster's anger was an inward kind. She knew how that worked from personal experience. Of course, when she tried to keep too much anger inside, things exploded *outside*.

What happens when people who can't smite hold in too much anger?

But if anything made sense as a means to calm oneself down, nature sounds would be it. Although she assumed the ones he listened to were more of the beach-at-sunset or late-autumn-forest-sunshower, not the mongoose-versus-rattlesnake or hippo-bulls-fighting-for-dominance that she would prefer. "Does it work?"

He shrugged. "So far, I suppose."

She sighed and flopped down in the chair facing his desk. "I guess it wouldn't matter if it failed and you killed yourself. I'd just bring you back."

He furrowed his brows at her. "Might I humbly request that you don't?" He paused, grimacing, and considered his words. "I saw the clip on the internet. It's, um, intense."

"That's one word for it."

"Want to talk about it?"

She did, and if this had been last week, she would have, but she still wasn't sure what to believe about him. Not that she thought Mrs. Thomas was lying, but people could get the wrong impression of others. As someone who was often accused of being the Antichrist, she understood that better than most. "Not really. But I think I've gotten politics out of my system."

"There's the silver lining." He started typing on his laptop, then said, "Okay, so no political science. Anything else interesting you? Maybe something less gruesome. Forensics?"

"I don't know. Do I have to know before I start college?"

"Oh, not at all. In fact, universities prefer if you come before you're ready and don't leave until after your first recommended colonoscopy."

She thought she knew what a colonoscopy was, but the casualness with which Mr. Foster mentioned it made her wonder if it wasn't something else. But then again, everything Mr. Foster said seemed casual.

God help me, I want to like him!

THEN LIKE HIM.

I wasn't talking to you.

SOUNDED LIKE YOU WERE.

"How about this," he said, turning the laptop toward her so she could see the screen. "Let's start with picking one of these dates for you to take the SAT, and then we'll just put off deciding the path for the rest of your life until, say, November."

"I guess that works." She stared at the computer screen, but none of the information was actually soaking in. Her eyes started to cross.

"Are you, um. Are you okay?" Mr. Foster stared at her with a soft, pained look she'd never seen him wear before.

"Yeah. I'm fine."

He shook his head minutely. "No. It would be insane if you were fine." He sighed and leaned back in his chair, bracing heavily on one of his arm rests as his eyes remained glued to her face. "You know, a few of your classmates live in abject poverty where they wouldn't get breakfast or lunch if they didn't come to school each day and they go hungry on the weekends. But if I didn't see from their paperwork that they qualified for free meals and that the only parent who stuck around has been on disability for five years, and if I didn't have to talk with the kids' CPS case managers and CASA volunteers, I'd never in a million years have guessed what the home life was like because they wear an expression a lot like the one you put on when you set foot in this building each day."

When he paused, Jessica wasn't sure what to say, so she stayed silent and Mr. Foster forged ahead. "Your paperwork doesn't list your father as God, and it doesn't mention that you're a genuine media shit magnet—excuse the language though there'll probably be more of it—but it doesn't have to because both of those things are about as public as they come. At least the poor kids can hide their secret behind FERPA.

"What I'm saying is that you have it hard, Jess. For the most part, you handle your business and keep it together.

God only knows how—maybe literally. But it's okay to ask people for help. And that includes me. If there's anything I can do to take some of the stress and confusion off your plate, you just—"

"Are you the Devil?"

Mr. Foster made a croaking sound in his throat, and she wasn't sure if it was a laugh or a gag. "The Devil?" He guffawed before reining it in. "No, Jessica, but thanks for asking. My ex-wife just went ahead and assumed."

"You're divorced?"

"Of course I'm divorced."

She was getting sidetracked. "How do I know you're not the Devil?" Her new, frank approach was based entirely on a whim, and she wasn't sure where to go from here.

"Um, well, because I'm too apathetic to be the Devil. Or maybe I'm too nice? No, probably not that one. I'm definitely too low on the totem pole. I can't imagine the Devil would subject himself to the job duties of a college counselor."

"Hmm … maybe not. But it could just be an excellent cover. No one expects the Devil to work in a high school."

"I'd argue with you on that account, but I see what you're getting at. So what do I need to do to convince you? Be overtly evil?" The faintest hint of a smirk wavered at the corner of his mouth.

She narrowed her eyes at him, feeling on unsteady ground. He raised an interesting point. "Possibly."

"So let me get this straight. All I have to do to convince you I'm *not* the Devil is, say, a ritual animal sacrifice. Would that suffice?"

The idea was so absurd, it managed to obliterate her suspicions. This was Mr. Foster. He was too placid to be the Devil but also not friendly enough to be the Devil. "Or maybe bomb an orphanage," she suggested.

Mr. Foster's eyes jolted wide and for a moment she thought she'd actually managed to offend him, which she didn't previously think was possible. But then he guffawed and stared at her wistfully with a small, contented smile lounging across his lips. "I almost can't believe it. You're just as dark as me. I mean, not Dark Prince-dark, but you know."

She nodded. "Yeah. I know. So you're not the Devil."

He shook his head. "Afraid not. Did you want me to be?"

"Nope. But if I've learned anything in life, it's that the Devil will be someone I don't want it to be. Wolf in sheep's clothing, and all that."

"Ah yes," he said thoughtfully, "the old sheep's clothing thing. Well"—he tugged on his sweater vest demonstratively—"I'm pretty sure this isn't wool, so"—he craned his neck around and stretched the vest's tag to where he could see it—"Oh shit. Well, it's a wool blend." He turned back toward her and shrugged apologetically. "I guess there's still room for debate."

Jessica relaxed the muscles in her shoulders, because she felt like she finally could for a little while, at least while she was in Mr. Foster's office. "I'm pretty sure *wool* isn't going to be the clue that tips me off, so don't worry. God would never make it that easy for me."

"And is there a specific reason why you feel the need to sleuth out the Devil?"

"I have to confront him. Maybe fight him."

"Ah." Mr. Foster rolled his shoulders and loosened his neck a bit. "All right. That's unfortunate. Well, first things first. Let's get you registered for the SAT."

* * *

Miranda's arms overflowed with crumpled up flyers as she stepped out of the McCloud house and onto the back porch, still in her sliding pants and T-shirt from softball practice. Jessica and Chris were already posted up in folding chairs, relaxing with a fresh Dos Equis each, courtesy of the woman of the house, and glanced up at the new arrival.

"So Mrs. Wurst has been busy," said Miranda, dumping the crinkled sheets onto the small patio table.

Jess leaned forward, grabbed one, and smoothed it out. "She really wants to start this church for me, doesn't she?"

"Of course she does," said Miranda irritably. "Everyone in this town wants to start their own freaking church." She plopped down into a chair facing Jess and Chris. He leaned back, reached his hand into the cooler, and pulled out a beer for Miranda, who accepted it gratefully. "These are just the flyers I found on the drive over here," she added.

"Jesus," Jessica muttered. "I guess some people are just a pain in the ass, no matter whether they're with you or against you."

"At least when she was your enemy, you could hate

her," Miranda said. "Now you can't be too mad at her. I mean, she seems to genuinely believe you're the messiah."

Jess sighed. "Yeah, well."

Football season was officially in full swing, and while she knew on an intellectual level that quitting the team was in everyone's best interest, maybe it wasn't that important. Or maybe the opportunity to resign hadn't presented itself in a pretty enough package yet. Or maybe people avoiding doing what they should all the time, so why should Jessica have to be any different? Plus, she was hard-pressed to think of anything more glorious than a post-conditioning beer, and she wasn't sure she was ready to lose this small indulgence yet.

Neither she nor Chris had bothered changing out of their practice gear, simply stripping down to their Under Armour shirts and athletic shorts. The weather had begun to shift into fall and cool gusts of air swept through the back covered patio, carrying the teenage sweat-stink out and away, allowing the trio to relax in their mesh fold-out chairs with built-in cup holders and stretch their legs out in front of them without fear of being smelled by the others.

"I think I need to get far away from this town," Miranda said before taking a swig from her beer.

The idea caught Jessica off balance. Where had that come from?

Chris didn't seem as put off by it, though. "Like how far? Dallas?"

"Maybe. Maybe farther."

Chris's eyebrows shot up. "Like Houston?"

Miranda shrugged. "I dunno. I had a recruiter from LSU come talk to me the other day."

Chris's jaw fell open at that. "You want to move out of Texas? All the way to *Louisiana?*"

Miranda narrowed her eyes at him. "Yeah, maybe. You know Louisiana is just one state over, right?"

"Psh, of course I know that." Chris quickly finished his first beer.

As he popped open another, Jessica asked, "Where are you thinking about going, Chris?"

It was a topic they'd danced around but never addressed: what happened if they went to different colleges? Broaching the subject with Miranda around felt somehow safer.

Chris seemed to consider his words carefully, which only made Jessica more nervous; Chris never considered his words carefully.

"I dunno. Been talking with a guy from Abilene Christian, one from Tech, one from Texas State, and one from SMU."

"Oh wow," Miranda said. "That's a lot of guys. All for football?"

Chris nodded.

Miranda turned to Jess. "Those are the same ones you've been talking to, right?"

"Eh, some of the same. Tech, A&M, UT, then a few others." She decided not to point out that the men from the Christian universities conspicuously passed her over, or that "a few others" really meant dozens—all of which were out of state. Destinee and Mr. Foster knew about the out of state ones, and she'd mentioned them to Miranda as the letters of interest came in, but always with a singular instruction: don't tell Chris. She wasn't sure how he'd take it, knowing places like Ohio State and USC were courting her but not him.

"What about all the out of state ones?" Miranda asked. "Like, didn't USC call you up the other day, just about ready to sign you then and there?"

Jess shot Miranda a pointed glare but could feel Chris's eyes glued to the side of her face. And then Miranda remembered. "Oh, wait. Maybe that was someone else."

Jessica sighed. "No, it was me." She turned toward Chris, and could tell he was attempting a poker face, but he wasn't great at it. His expression was simply slack, like he was falling asleep. "You okay?" she asked.

He blinked rapidly and nodded as he looked away.

"Well hey," Miranda said, "you two could end up at the same place. Wouldn't that be fun if you got to play football together in college?"

"Yeah," Jess said without looking at Chris.

"Yeah," Chris said without looking at Jess.

Time for a new subject. This had entered into territory Jess didn't care to explore any further. So she turned the conversation to a topic that was easier to discuss. "You know, I think that assassination attempt might have been intended for me."

She'd given the notion plenty of thought before saying those words aloud, fearing that it would sound a little egocentric to assume that someone wanted to kill her more than Jameson, even though it wasn't much of a stretch to assume that people who thought she was the Antichrist might want to see her dead.

Miranda and Chris avoided her eyes uncomfortably, then finally Miranda said, "Yeah, we were thinking the same thing."

"We just didn't want you to be all freaked out," Chris added.

"Wait. We? Y'all have been talking about this?"

Miranda and Chris glanced at each other. "Yeah, but, like, not much," Miranda said.

"Just right after it came on the news," Chris added. "I mean, who would want to kill Jameson Fractal anyway? He's dreamy ... or whatever."

Jess took a sip and leaned back farther in her chair. "He's a lot less dreamy when he has a bullet hole through his head, I can tell you that."

"I still think you should've gone to see him in the hospital the next day," Miranda said for what had to be the twentieth time since the incident. "Wendy said he wanted to see you. You know, sometimes when someone saves someone else's life, the two fall in love." She paused, then, "Oh, sorry, Chris."

"Listen, if Jessica left me for Jameson Fractal, I would understand. Dude's a stud. He got insanely ripped for that movie that came out last year. What was it called? Jack ..."

"Jack ..." Miranda supplied, also trying to remember the title.

"Hoffman?"

Miranda locked eyes with him. "Jack Hoffman? That *can't* be right."

Chris shook his head. "No, but it's something like that. Jack something."

"Yeah," Miranda agreed. "Jack something."

"Point is, he was ripped. I wouldn't even be mad if you left me for him."

"Okay." Jess waved her hand through the air to get them back on track. "First of all, I'm not going to end up with Jameson. I doubt I'll ever even have another sex dream about him, after seeing his face like that. Second of all, we don't know that the reason he wanted to see me was to thank me. He could've just as easily wanted to blame me for getting him shot. But mostly, I just don't know that I want to meet him again. Like, you can't make much of a worse first impression with someone than to be the last person they saw before they died. For all we know, he could've just started screaming when he saw my face and not stopped till he was sedated. I don't think I could handle that."

"That's true," said Chris.

Miranda smacked his arm. "No, it's not." She turned to Jess. "That wouldn't have happened. But it was your choice to see him or not, and he's fine now."

"Besides the psychological trauma," Jess said.

"Right." Miranda paused. "Besides the psychological trauma."

Filming for the third of the Ravaged series, starring Jameson Fractal, had been slated to start the week after Jessica's endorsement, but it'd been over a month, and Jameson still hadn't left his Austin condo. At least that was the rumor (which was substantiated by Wendy Peterman).

It sounded like he was going through some sort of metamorphosis, and who even knew how he would emerge on the other side. Jess knew better than to hope for anything good, considering the transformation Mrs. Wurst had gone through post-resurrection. Now every time Jessica thought about her celebrity crush, she felt a pang of guilt in her stomach followed by a brief wave of nausea.

Miranda leaned over quickly and pulled her cell phone from the back pocket of her softball pants. After fiddling with it, she said, "Gotta go. Alicia Alejo won't get off my ass about finishing our government project." She tipped back the last of her beer. "Guess she does have a point. I gotta graduate before I can go to college."

"It does help, I've heard." Jess reached forward and took the empty from Miranda before tossing it into the recycling bin behind them.

Once Miranda had left through the side gate, Jess turned to Chris. "You have homework, too?" It was getting late, probably close to nine, and the sun had disappeared, but it wasn't yet completely dark.

"Yeah, but I can do it later."

He didn't want to leave yet. Jess understood. She didn't want him to leave yet either. It felt like there were things to talk about, but she wasn't quite ready to bring them up.

Chris did her the favor of starting off conversation. "I've been noticing strange things lately."

"Huh?"

"Like, um, feelings."

This was *not* what she was expecting. She couldn't imagine there was a good scenario where a boyfriend told his girlfriend he was experiencing strange feelings. *Stay calm!* "Okay?"

"It's just like, when I look at people ... I don't know how to say it." He scooted back in his chair, leaning forward, staring out across the McCloud back yard and beyond the chain-link fence to the Del Toros' back yard, which was cluttered with a rotation of random objects Jess could never definitively identify. "So like, the other day. I was looking at Enrique, and I just ... felt something."

Oh. Shit.

If it'd been anyone but Enrique Gutierrez, a sophomore who was way hotter than should be allowed for a fifteen-year-old, Jessica might not have come to the conclusion that she did. But it *was* Enrique, with his perfectly symmetrical face, his lean soccer physique, his chiseled jaw and dimples and eyes that welled up with passion every time he spoke about his childhood in Guatemala.

"Okay," Jess said hesitantly. She wasn't experienced with this sort of thing, but she knew better than to make Chris feel guilt or shame—a lesson she'd learned from Greg, actually.

Freaking Greg.

"And it was the same thing with Quentin. And a few others. The same— I don't know what to call it."

"It's okay," she said. "I don't think what you're feeling is that odd, actually."

Chris's eyes lit up and he jerked his head toward her. "You don't? You know what I'm feeling?"

"Well, I don't understand it personally, but I've heard of it. I mean, it's normal. And God's okay with it, actually."

"Huh? Why wouldn't God be okay with it?"

Jess laughed. "Right? I don't know why everyone says it's a sin. It's really not."

Dammit! Dammit! Dammit! Why? Why did I have to fall for a gay?!

"Who says it's a sin?" Chris asked, squinting intensely at her.

"It doesn't matter. It's not."

Chris cocked his head to the side and narrowed his eyes. "Wait. *What's* not?"

"Being ..." she looked at him. What was going on here? "Being gay."

Chris's arms flung back, spilling beer down his front. He cursed and wiped away the liquid before looking back up at Jessica. "I'm not gay. No, that's not even— That's not at all what I was saying. I mean, I'm glad God's cool with it, but damn, Jess. You thought ... ? Fuuuck. "

"Wait, then what were you saying about Enrique and Quentin?"

"The colors," he said plainly.

"I don't think you're supposed to call them that."

"No. I mean"—he paused, shut his eyes tight, crinkling his nose, and then finally had the words for it—"I see colors. Around people."

"You what?" She set her beer in the cup holder of the chair so it didn't fall out of her grasp.

"Colors. It's this weird thing. I've ... sort of always seen them, here and there, and I guess I kinda figured everyone did but that it was one of those things like sex and addiction and gun control that nobody's supposed to talk about with others. But lately I've been seeing it pretty much constantly with certain people. The ones around Enrique are just the strongest I've seen in a while."

"Ah." So that explained nothing.

"I mean, it's probably just a brain thing, right? I've had a few concussions. And then the weird dreams ... that's just a brain thing, too."

"Right," Jess said, unsure of what else to say. "A brain thing. Probably just a brain thing."

"You think I should get it checked out?"

She shrugged. "If you want to. Maybe it's just your retinas or ..." She shook her head vaguely as she tried to think of some similar ability in the animal kingdom and came up short.

"You don't think I'm crazy, do you?" he asked.

"Of course not." She chuckled. "I'm just glad you're not gay."

"Me too." He reached his hand out for hers and she took it. "Me fuckin' too."

"Grab me another, would you?" she said, wiggling her bottle at him. She downed the rest as he let go of her hand and reached back into the cooler.

It was now or never. They were already talking openly, which they hadn't had a good chance to do in a while, and Chris wasn't gay. She had momentum, basically.

When he handed her the beer, she went for it. "Hey, can I ask you something?" She couldn't look at him.

"Of course."

"Are you mad that we haven't ... you know."

"Made love?"

She snorted and looked up at him. Oh, he was being genuine. "Uh, yeah. That."

"No, I'm not mad about it."

She looked back down at her beer bottle. "I mean, would you want to?"

"Would I want to?!" he echoed incredulously. "Uh, getting nasty with you in the bed of my truck—"

"Well, it doesn't have to be there—"

"—Is all I think about."

"That's *all* you think about?"

He shrugged. "Well, okay, no. That and football. Those two things."

"Then why aren't you mad that we haven't yet?"

Now it was his turn to dodge eye contact. "I don't think your Father would approve."

"Uh. I don't think that matters."

He clutched the arms of his chair like he was holding himself in place. "Of course it matters!"

"Okay, so maybe it matters a little bit."

Chris leaned toward her and whispered, "He could smite me for it."

"He can hear whispers, Chris, and I don't think He has much room to judge, considering my mom was a few months younger than I am right now when He ... you know."

He still didn't seem convinced. "Maybe."

"I mean, I can talk to Him."

Chris set his jaw and nodded. "Yeah, do that. But don't tell him I wanted you to. I don't want him to think I'm pressuring you. Because I'm not. Really, it's okay."

Jessica sighed. Poor Chris. "Okay, I won't tell Him."

Chris seemed appeased, and he slapped the armrests of his chair. "I should get home."

"Yeah."

As he stood, so did she. "Want to make out a little first?" she asked.

"Hell yeah, girl. You. Me. Backseat of my truck. Right now!" He reached down, scooping her up with an arm under her shoulder blade and one under her knees, and carried her hurriedly through the house toward the front door, darting by Destinee, who sat on the couch watching TV and shouted distractedly as they passed, "Use protection!"

Chapter Thirteen

The away game against Andrews High had made it a late night for Jessica. Normally, that wouldn't be an issue, but this was not a normal Saturday morning. This was the SATs, a high-stakes game of academics, where the winners were showered in scholarships while the losers were left to research which community college they wanted to drop out of in the next couple years.

Jessica dragged herself through the front doors of Mooremont and groggily headed toward the testing classroom to see if she couldn't sneak in a quick nap in the hallway before they were allowed inside.

Chris was already there when she turned the corner and saw the long line of students, all of whom appeared to have fallen against the wall and slid straight down, their knees tucked up toward their chest, many still wearing their backpacks.

When he saw her, he used his shoulder to shove Drew

Fenster away from him, creating a small space for Jessica to slide down the wall next to him.

"Hey."

"Hey."

He wove his fingers through hers and let their clasped hands fall limp between them without another word said. Jessica closed her eyes.

She tried to stay focused on the test ahead, but her brain was too foggy, and before long her mind began crafting fractal patterns of thought, each one branching out into some other more nonsensical topic, until she lost all awareness of where she was in space and time.

"Miss McCloud," said a familiar voice that was way too alert for the hour. Jess's eyes shot open and she realized her mouth had been gaping. She looked up and spotted Mrs. Thomas, who was heading down the hallway in her direction. "You have a minute?"

"Of course."

She pulled her fingers gently away from Chris (also sitting with his eyes closed, mouth gaping) and followed the principal farther down the hall until they were out of earshot of the others. "You eat breakfast?" Mrs. Thomas asked.

"I had an orange."

Mrs. Thomas pressed her lips together tightly to hold back whatever disapproval Jess knew she probably deserved. "Here." She held out a granola bar. "From the cafeteria."

"Thanks."

"How are you feeling this morning?"

"Nervous, I guess."

Mrs. Thomas smiled. "Don't be. You'll do fine. In fact, I imagine you're probably the student with the top chance of a perfect score. But, between you and me, if you find that you know the answers to *all* the questions, maybe just omit one or two so ... you know."

"Colleges don't think I used God powers?"

"Right." Mrs. Thomas winked. "Other than that, I just wanted to check in. I know we haven't spoken since the assassination."

Mrs. Thomas's willingness to call it what it was—unlike most other people who skirted around the brutal truth with things like "incident" and "endorsement thing"— brought Jessica to a higher level of alertness immediately. "And I just wanted to make sure you're doing okay. That's a lot of trauma for someone your age to go through."

"Yeah, I suppose so. I'm fine."

Mrs. Thomas cocked an eyebrow. "Really? You know you can tell me."

Jessica sighed. "I mean, it sucks. And if I'm being honest, the more I think about it, the less I believe that bullet was intended for him."

Mrs. Thomas nodded, apparently getting Jessica's meaning immediately. "I was wondering if you'd come to that conclusion. I have my concerns as well. It was incredibly brave of you not to run off the stage before the area had been secured."

"Huh?"

"Oh, well, just ... you know. One person was shot by an unknown gunman, who, for all we know could've fired off a few rounds without any trouble, but rather than ducking for cover, you ran to help the wounded."

"Oh. Huh. I didn't even consider that."

Mrs. Thomas tilted her head to the side and smiled. "Well, not sparing a thought for your personal safety is part of bravery, I suppose. And I wouldn't expect you to worry about it, seeing as how you have someone watching out for you."

"Who?" Then, "Oh, right." She really should have gone straight to bed after the game. She fidgeted with the granola bar wrapper. "I can't help but wonder if I'm not endangering all the people around me every time I go out in the open."

Mrs. Thomas nodded sympathetically but said nothing.

"Last night, at the Andrews game, I thought I saw a sniper crouched on top of the announcer's box. I almost had a heart attack. Turned out it was just a big vulture."

"Yeah, that town is full of those awful things."

"They still haven't caught him," she mumbled. She didn't like thinking about it. And she didn't want others to know she thought about it, but Mrs. Thomas felt safe enough.

The principal placed a warm, comforting hand on Jessica's shoulder. "They'll catch him. They always do. It's just a matter of time."

"Sure, but in the meantime, am I endangering everyone around me when I'm on the field? And what about other people who want to snipe me and have terrible aim? I mean, sure, I can always bring people back to life, but I don't want to have to resurrect my friends whenever a sniper misses."

Mrs. Thomas appeared concerned now. "Yes, if I'm being perfectly candid, I do worry about your safety when you're exposed like that."

Jessica decided to give a voice to the concern that'd been circling in her mind for long weeks since the assassination. "Do you think I should quit football?"

She'd come up with no definitive decision herself, and each time the thought cycled back through to the front of her mind, she'd begun to experience a stark pain behind her eyes and a kick of nausea. She didn't want to have to think about it anymore. She was willing to do whatever Mrs. Thomas suggested, and while part of her hoped the woman said it wasn't necessary, most of her was looking for the validation she needed to do what she already knew was right.

"I know you love football, Jessica. But if you feel like your life is in danger when you play it, then I think you already know what you should do. There's more to life than football, anyway." Then she quickly added, "Don't tell anyone I said that. The athletic booster club would have my ass. They've been after me all year, saying I hate sports and don't understand their value."

"Do they know about how you ordered special football pads for me? That's not something someone who hates sports does."

"Uh ... no. They don't know about that. I had to fudge some numbers for it, so it's best if they don't find out."

Jess sighed and wondered if there'd ever come a day when Mrs. Thomas got sick of taking a bullet for her.

Maybe not the best metaphor.

"Anything else weighing heavy on your mind?" asked her principal.

"No," said Jess. "Just the usual."

Mrs. Thomas smiled. "Well, no one said being a teenager was easy. Good luck today. Not that you need luck." Then she turned and headed down the hallway, leaving Jessica alone with her mind finally made up on at least one thing.

It was time to officially retire from football.

* * *

For as much as football took over Jessica's life in the late summer to late fall, it wasn't until Coach Rex started spending most of his free time at the McCloud doublewide before televised football was integrated into the weekend soundtrack of Jessica's home life.

After Chris dropped her off following the SATs, refusing her offer to come inside because, "My brain is melting, and I don't want to say something stupid in front of your mom," Jess wandered inside, her brain feeling not unlike Chris had described his, and was greeted by the sound of college football and the sight of her mother and Coach Rex making out on the couch.

THIS GUY.

Stop being jealous.

NOT JEALOUS. DISDAINFUL. THE MAN TEACHES HIGH

SCHOOL GEOGRAPHY AND HE THINKS NIGER IS PRONOUNCED—

Is Coach Rex the Devil?

And God's voice was gone.

"I'm home," she said, standing five feet from where they were tangled together. Coach Rex jerked away from Destinee and cleared his throat.

"Oh, how'd it go, baby?" Destinee asked, not bothering to fix her mussed hair.

"Fine."

It was now or never.

"Hey, Coach, can I talk to you?" In the minutes between when she'd triple checked her answers for each section of the test and when the time had actually run out, Jessica had firmly made up her mind about quitting the football team.

And had long conversations with her Father about how she absolutely did *not* want him to double-check her answers. Not even the obligatory ones she omitted to avoid looking like a cheater (though God insisted that giving her the answers was not actually cheating since He was part of her in a way they both agreed was a little creepy).

Coach Rex looked at her like he was a guilty child who'd been expecting this lecture for quite some time.

"Don't worry," she said, "it's not about"—she motioned at him and her mother—"that. It's about football."

"Ah," he said, looking relieved for only a moment before appearing even more concerned than before. "What about football?"

She knew he wouldn't take it well, but she'd prepped

herself for that. And so had God, who hadn't approved of the idea of her hanging up one of her miracles, but whose monotone voice took on a novel hint of enthusiasm when it came time to mull over how she would break the news to her coach.

"I quit."

"Quit what?" asked Rex, his face showing no signs of understanding.

"Football. I'm quitting the team."

The words still didn't seem to make sense to him. "You need a break from it? That's fine. Take a week off. You've been working hard."

"No, I quit. Like, I'm done. Mulroney is a great backup kicker. I'm sure he'll be able to—"

"Mulroney is one poorly timed sneeze away from failing all his classes at any given point." Rex's face had turned the dark shade of red that she'd only ever seen on him during summer afternoon conditioning. "What in Sam Hill are you talking about, McCloud?"

She wasn't sure how to put it any plainer. "I don't want to play football anymore."

"Now, that just can't be right," said Rex. "Didn't you say not a week ago that football was the only thing getting you out of bed this school year?"

"I mean, yeah, but you know, things chan—"

Coach Rex held up a hand, stopping her before she could finish. "Listen. I don't pretend to understand women. So I won't try to make sense of this. You're gonna do what you're gonna do, and of course I think this is a mistake. You're the top kicker in the state, and probably in the country, if any of those no-gooders in them basketball states bothered to keep stats like they knew how to count past ten, but if you think you need to quit for whatever reason, I'm gonna support you on that."

"O-okay. Um. Thanks. Yeah, I'm still quitting."

He nodded, and Jess assumed it was okay for her to leave. So she did, heading toward her bedroom, but not before she heard her mother, who'd stayed unbelievably quiet throughout the conversation, say, "You handled that so well, Rex. God, you're a stud." Jess scurried into her room and shut the door just as the moaning and scuffling began again in the living room.

* * *

Jessica had a difficult time remembering what she used to do after school before football practice was a staple in her life.

She'd finished all her homework before Jeopardy had even started, watched two back-to-back episodes, rewatched a documentary on dolphin pod behavior, microwaved herself a meal—Destinee was still at the pharmacy—and now she was left scratching her head. Maybe she could draw something?

Man, I really am bored.

Drawing had been a much avoided pastime since she'd accidentally seen into God's mind and drawn Ms. Rickles being sexed up ("porn-style" as Jess considered it) by Chief Wurst. The image still hung around Jessica's brain like a memory of a scene she'd actually stumbled into at age five.

She wondered if counseling might help. She'd consider it, if she weren't convinced she'd run any counselor out of the room screaming—or worse, praying—within a half hour.

So she parked it on the couch and began surfing the channels. Surely not everything on TV at this time of evening consisted of people making poor decisions.

Nope. Everything did.

The front door burst open to her right, and she had only a split second to chide herself for not locking it while she was home alone before her mind was distracted by the sight of Christopher Riley stepping inside, face still red from ... exertion? Or was he really that pissed?

"What the shit is this I hear about you quitting the team?"

Okay, so not exertion.

Jess tensed. She'd expected him to be disappointed, sure, but not livid. "Yeah. I, uh, I quit."

"What the hell?"

"What?"

He shut the door behind him, not slamming it, but definitely not gentle about it either. "When were you going to tell me?"

"I didn't know I needed to tell you directly."

His jaw fell open. "Are you— Are you fucking serious with that? You didn't think you needed to tell the quarterback of the team that you were quitting?"

"Ohhh," Jess said, something about his last words hitting a nerve and igniting her own temper. "Here I was thinking you were upset because you were my boyfriend, but really you don't care about *me*, you just care about whether the team wins state again. Fine. I'll tell you directly, teammate to teammate." She puffed up her shoulders, and lowered her voice. "Hey, *dude*, just wanted to let you know that I'm quitting the team, *bro*." She relaxed her posture and flashed a saccharine smile. "That better?"

Chris blinked, confused. "What the fuck was that?"

"*That*," she said emphatically, "was your kicker letting you know she's quitting the team in a language you understand."

Still, he seemed confused. He narrowed his eyes at her. "I don't say bro," he said reflectively. He shook off the thought. "Why are you quitting anyway?"

"Oh geez, Chris. Maybe because I don't want to have to resurrect everyone on the goddamn field when another sniper shows up. And maybe I don't want to push my luck that every sniper who comes after me will have the aim of a drunk with vertigo."

"You really think God's going to let you get sniped?"

Jess let Chris's words hang in the air, hoping he'd realize what he'd just said.

"I *absolutely* think God would let me get sniped, if the timing was right to prove one of His *Big Points*. Ever heard of a guy named Jesus, Chris?"

Chris cocked his head to the side. "Wait, did he get sniped? I thought ... I'm pretty sure they didn't have guns back then. Could a slingshot—"

"No, he didn't get sniped by a slingshot, but God didn't exactly protect him from getting his ass handed to him. Sniping him would've been a mercy, compared to letting him get crucified."

"Well then maybe that's it!" said Chris, like he'd just made a breakthrough. "Maybe you don't have to worry about being sniped at a football game because it would be too swift and merciful of a death for God to allow it."

"Is that supposed to reassure me?"

"Jess." He crossed the living room and sat on the edge of the couch, turning toward her where she sat. "I just don't understand this. You love football. You love the team. Kicking is your miracle. What made you want to turn your back on it all, really?"

"It's just that there's more to life than football."

Chris moaned and wiped his hand over his face. "Mrs. Thomas. That's what you were talking to her about before the SATs."

"What?" How'd he know?

"She says those exact words at every athletic booster club meeting."

Oh right. Mrs. Riley was the president of the athletic booster club.

Then Chris added, "She just hates sports."

"She does not!"

"Clearly she does. No one that large can love sports."

"Chris!"

"What? It's true."

"What about Damien? He's humongous and that's why he makes a fantastic linebacker."

Chris waved that away. "Please, Damien looks like he wants to slit his wrists after every practice. Dude hates sports more than anyone I know. You can see it in the dark pits of his eyes."

"Doesn't matter. Mrs. Thomas doesn't hate sports, she just sees the perspective of it. You even said yourself once that my life is bigger than football. So why don't I get to quit?"

"First of all, your life *is* bigger than football. I stand by that, but that doesn't mean football isn't an important part of it. Mrs. Thomas has never supported you in—"

Jess jumped up from the couch, causing Chris to follow suit. "Mrs. Thomas is the only person who's ever supported *me.*"

"That's a load of steaming horseshit, and you know it, Jess."

She knew she'd crossed a line, but she was too angry to care. "It's not. Everyone supports the daughter of God, but when the daughter of God actually makes a decision for herself, ohhh nooo, she doesn't know what she's doing. Mrs. Thomas is the only one who has ever gotten that … And Greg."

Chris's eyebrows shot up and he laughed dryly. "Greg? Really? You think he gave two shits about you? Is that why he let Sandra blow him the same night you broke up with him?"

"Wait, what?"

"Please, Jess. That's a shit argument. Greg and Mrs. Thomas? You really want to side with them over me and your mom and Coach Rex and a whole team of people who care about you?"

She threw her hands on her hips. "What's your problem with Mrs. Thomas anyway? Is it because you were never her favorite?"

Chris opened his mouth to say something but then shut it again and chuckled, puffing from his nose as he shook his head. "You know, fine. Quit the team. It's a huge mistake. You know it. I know it. But fuck it, right? Fuck all of it. Fuck the support the team's given you, fuck that you love it, fuck that Jesus told you it's what you're supposed to be doing, fuck that God is a fan. Fuck it all." He turned and walked toward the front door, opening it before pausing in the doorway.

He turned and threw one last look at Jessica, scowling slightly. "You remember the day you smote the bird in kindergarten?"

Jess said nothing.

"I never told you what Mrs. Thomas said to me and Trent." His eyes traveled up to the far ceiling as he recalled the words. "She said that we'd been marked. Marked by God. That He would remember this forever, and it was only a matter of time before we met the same fate as the grackle, that we couldn't avoid it. That it was how we'd die some day, and all we could do was push back the inevitable by being nice to you. And if we pushed it, if we were too mean … poof." His expression grew more disgusted. "Who says that to a five year old?"

He turned and shut the door, and Jess was left alone, feeling a heat grow behind her eyes, wondering what in her Father's name had just happened.

She didn't get long to think about it, though. She could still hear the faintest sound of the F-350's engine lugging down the street when her phone started ringing from the kitchen where she'd left it.

She missed the call by two steps, and when she looked down at her cell, she knew immediately something was wrong. A total of nine missed calls from Miranda, Wendy, Maria, and a number with a Midland area code that Jessica didn't recognize. On top of that were twelve texts waiting to be read.

She scrolled through them.
From Miranda:

WTF!?

Did you see the news?

Call me.

Jess, are you okay?

Please just call or text to let me know you're okay.

From Wendy:

Just heard. Don't answer any calls from people you don't know.

Actually, don't answer any calls.

Except from me. Answer my calls.

Call me when you get this. Don't talk to anyone before you talk to me.

From Maria:

Eugene Thornton's source checks out. Call me if you need anything.

From Destinee:

Do we have tampons?

I feel like we're out of tampons.

I bought tampons. Home soon.

So there was no way this was anything but terrible news. Except the tampon part. They could always use more tampons.

Jessica tried to piece together the clues. Eugene Thornton had exposed something. Apparently it was a crisis that might result in Jessica not being okay. There was still so much information missing.

I suppose this is what the internet's good for.

She pulled up the browser on her phone and searched for *Eugene Thornton, news, Jessica McCloud*, and then clicked on the most recent headline.

It appeared that Channel 6 had seen fit to give Eugene his own blog where he could fling slime whenever he wanted without the limitations of television programming and scheduling.

The blog's banner was a picture of his stupid face with

his stupid mustache and stupid eyebrows and that stupid hat he always wore.

God, he's so stupid.

AMEN.

Hey! You're here! Should I read this article?

THOU SHALT.

You don't have to be so pushy.

The headline at the top was about all she needed to read, though:

Staged Assassination Casts Doubt on Midland Mayor, Second Coming of Christ

"Shitballs." She started to read and got so far as to make it through the horrific opening line (*What would Jesus do? He wouldn't have helped assassinate one of the country's most beloved celebrities to use his resurrection powers for political gain.*) before the phone vibrated in her hand and began ringing. Wendy was giving it another shot, it seemed.

Jessica answered. "Hello?"

"Oh thank God. Have you spoken to anyone?"

"About Eugene?"

"So you've heard. Okay. But have you spoken to anyone?"

"No. I was just reading the story when you—"

"Good. Don't talk to anyone. I should be there in an hour."

"Can I talk to my mom about it?"

There was silence on the other end. "Probably better if you don't. Let me tell her when I get there. That way she won't go do something rash."

"She'll still try, whether you're here or not." At least Wendy had Destinee pegged.

"I can handle it."

Jessica recalled Wendy's toned arms and sculpted calves that were left uncovered whenever she opted for a pencil skirt over her usual flowy pants and then she remembered the way the woman had been able to lift her onto her feet from where she'd crouched over Jameson.

Wendy definitely had the muscle necessary to wrestle Destinee to the ground. Hopefully she had the street smarts too, because Jessica knew from having witnessed it that Destinee wasn't above a cheap shot if that's what it took to win.

"Maria said Eugene Thornton's sources were solid. Is that true?"

The panic in Wendy's voice was incredibly disconcerting. "I thought you hadn't talked to anyone."

"I haven't. She just texted me. I haven't replied."

"Phew. Okay. Good. Don't. And yes, it looks like for once Eugene didn't have to pull a story out of his ass. He actually got a good one. Although he did guess at a few things."

"What do you mean?"

"Well"—she seemed to be considering her words carefully, which was no surprise for a PR rep, Jess supposed—"he said the Cox campaign was responsible for the assassination and that Polly Cox *did* have knowledge of the plan prior to it happening, which, turns out, is true. Or at least verified by the shooter."

"They caught him?" A weight lifted from her shoulders.

"Yes, but hold up before you get excited. In typical fashion, Eugene Thornton has added a bit of his own flourish to the narrative."

"Of course." And here it came. She could sense the doom before it hit. "What's he saying?"

"Well, he says his sources also name you as a coconspirator."

* * *

The McCloud home was well stocked with tampons by the time Wendy Peterman arrived an hour later. It had taken all of Jessica's amateurish acting skills to keep from tipping her mother off to the truth that something terrible was unfolding.

Destinee had been so exhausted from working two hours later than she'd intended, covering for one of her coworkers who "can't take one day off being a worthless sack of shit to get to work on time" and was therefore oblivious to the obvious signs that something wasn't right.

Firstly, Jessica was watching *The Bachelorette*. It had been a calculated choice, make no mistake. Destinee McCloud would never turn off *The Bachelorette* to see what was happening in the rest of the world.

But Jessica would never turn on *The Bachelorette* for any reason other than to distract her mother. It was a move so obvious, Jess wondered if it would immediately tip off Destinee that something wasn't right, but thankfully, she was too tired to pick up on it and was likely grateful to be saved the energy of deciding how to spend her night.

The second obvious clue was that Jessica immediately offered to go plug in her mother's phone so it could charge. Of course she didn't mention she would also turn the phone to silent and leave it in the cramped laundry room, which Destinee only ever used on Sunday evenings while cursing herself for having forgotten to do the laundry for the upcoming week.

But Destinee had accepted the offer without a second thought. "Thanks, baby. I mean, I've had a *day*. Nice to be pampered a bit. Maybe you can teach Rex how this works."

It was right after Destinee had asked how her day was and Jessica responded with "Wonderful!" that she thought she'd definitely pushed the charade too far. Surely Destinee would know she was lying and covering up something, with an answer as positive as that; Jessica hadn't had a wonderful day in all her life.

Even still, Destinee simply looked at her daughter curiously for a moment, then nodded. "Good. Didn't miss football?"

"Nope. Not at all."

"Maybe you made the right choice then."

Phew. Another bullet dodged.

Jessica grabbed two beers from the fridge and brought them into the living room, handing one over to her mother before flopping down on the couch as well. "Hey, Wendy is coming over in a little, but it's no big deal. Just a check in."

Destinee bolted upright where she sat. "Like hell it ain't! What's happened?"

Shit.

"Nothing, Mom. Everything's fine."

Destinee narrowed her eyes at Jessica. "Ahh ... I see what's going on here. You being all helpful, having a 'wonderful' day, watching *The Bachelorette*! Something's *real* fucked up, ain't it?" She fumbled with the remote, and Jessica knew she would be sunk as soon as her mother landed on a news station. One of them was bound to be covering the assassination scandal.

But the local news had already finished, and before Destinee could find where Jessica had plugged in her phone, there was a knock on the front door.

Jessica sprinted over and let Wendy inside.

"What the shit is going on?" Destinee demanded, charging into the living room from the kitchen, clutching her Shiner but otherwise empty handed. "I got a bug-out bag in my closet. Do we need the bug-out bag?"

"No, no," Wendy said calmly, motioning for Destinee to relax. She shot a what-did-I-tell-you glance at Jess. "It looks bad, but we're going to get it under control quickly."

"She doesn't actually know," Jess said.

Wendy sighed. "Ah. Okay. Mrs. McCloud, would you mind making us some tea?"

"Tea?" Destinee echoed, confused. "Like Lipton?"

Wendy flinched minutely. "Sure. Lipton sounds fine."

Once they were seated around the kitchen table and Wendy had filled Destinee in on the basics, pausing occasionally to assure her that it really was best for everyone if they came up with a plan before "kicking all those politicians' asses," the Lipton had finished brewing.

"I'll just take mine hot," Wendy said, when Destinee began emptying the ice tray into three glasses.

Destinee eyed her like she was crazy. "Okay then." She switched out one of the glasses with a coffee cup. "You want sweet or unsweet?"

Wendy had to think about that. "Do you have any honey?"

"Honey?" Destinee echoed. "Uh. Maybe. But it's gonna be old." She headed to the pantry and began digging through. "How long does honey last before it expires?"

"Thousands of years at least," Wendy said.

Destinee's head shot out of the pantry, and she looked at her daughter.

Jess nodded.

"All right," Destinee said, "whatever you say, but that sure doesn't sound right."

Destinee brought over two iced teas and one hot cup of Lipton with honey and sat down across from Wendy, who looked at Jess. "Oh, Jameson sends his regards."

"Crap! Does he think I was in on shooting him?"

"No, no. Well, I mean, at first, yeah. I convinced him otherwise, though. He gets it. You were both similarly exploited by Cox. I gave him your number and he said he'd call. I hope you don't mind."

"Yeah, that's fine." Jess slipped her phone from her pocket, scrolled down the list of missed calls, and found the unknown number, then saved it as *Jameson Fractal?* just in case.

"Are you checking Facebook?" Wendy asked. She didn't sound mad.

"No."

"Oh. I was just going to say that you might want to

release a statement on all your social media channels, one we'd compose together, obviously. And I forgot to mention that I was looking for you on a few different ones, and couldn't find you. We really need to up your SEO and get you some followers, otherwise you'll never have the necessary visibility for a successful platform."

"Um." Jess didn't know how to break the news to Wendy. She knew the PR rep wouldn't be thrilled about it. "I don't actually ... I'm not on social media."

"Oh sure," Wendy replied understandingly. "So like, you have a personal Facebook account, but you haven't created an official page? Or like, you Snapchat, but it's under an alias?"

"No. See—"

Destinee took it from there. "She tried the Facebook thing in junior high, and it didn't work out so great with the cyberbullying and all that."

Wendy chuckled, wide-eyed as if she thought she were being played. "Well, *every*one's cyberbullied. That's just part of it." She paused, and her smile faded. "So wait, are you telling me— You mean to say you don't actually— I couldn't find you on Twitter because—" Slowly it dawned on the poor woman. A sharp intake of air caused her to choke, and she gulped down her tea, cringing around the taste, to regain control of her breathing.

Jessica shot a concerned glance at Destinee, who shook her head minutely and mouthed, "It's fine."

Eventually Wendy was able to speak again. "You don't have *any* social media presence?"

"I have an email address I use for school stuff," Jessica supplied lamely.

Wendy laughed, then her face went slack, then she laughed again. "You have an email address."

"Yeah."

"Okay. I guess that's where we start." She popped her knuckles and rolled her neck in slow circles. "What's your email address?"

"MexicanKicker7 at hot—"

"No."

"Huh?"

Wendy looked like she was going to be sick. "Just ... Please stop." She shut her eyes and massaged her temples. "Okay. This is worse than I thought. We'll have to start from scratch. God. MexicanKicker?" She took three deep breaths, and then opened her eyes and sat up straight again. "Listen, Polly Cox's poll numbers are about to tank. The only reason I say, 'about to' is because there hasn't been enough time to poll people yet. But it's not going to be good, come tomorrow."

Jess felt despair congeal in her stomach. "But that means Jimmy will win."

Wendy nodded. "By default, yes. Probably. But I don't do PR for Polly Cox. She's not my problem, thank God. I just have to worry about you right now, and you need to distance yourself from all of this as quickly as possible. You need to take control of your narrative."

"Meaning?" Destinee asked.

"Meaning," said Wendy, "that we have a lot of work to do to get your social media branding up and running before people wake up tomorrow. You need to take back your story from the hands of the masses."

"That sounds like a lot of work," Jessica said. Her mind drifted back to being bored earlier that evening, and she wished she'd enjoyed that more while it lasted.

Wendy was already busy though, typing away on a tablet she'd pulled from her large purse. "Do you own your domain name?"

"I have no idea what that means."

Wendy blinked quickly three times. "Okay. Wow. Um. Let's start small. Destinee, go grab me whatever baby photos of Jessica you have. And we'll need more coffee. Jessica, start writing down your thoughts in one hundred and forty character chunks—"

"Why?"

"Just do it," Wendy snapped. "Trust me. I know what I'm doing here. When it comes to social media, less you ask why, the better you'll be at it."

"But what do I write about?"

Wendy waved her hand vaguely in the air before jabbing at her tablet. "Whatever. Things you like, things that interest you."

"Like giraffes?"

Finally Wendy seemed to approve as she smiled at Jessica. "Giraffes. Perfect." She hesitated. "You're pro-giraffe, right?"

"God. Of course. Who's not—"

"Good. We don't need to add PETA to this cluster."

So as Destinee returned with a tub of baby pictures and Wendy began calling her favorite web developers, Jessica took to writing down her thoughts in one hundred and forty characters or fewer, starting with, *Wish I could be at the zoo right now. I wonder what the giraffes are up to? Ugh. Gonna be a late night.*

And it was.

Chapter Fourteen

"I swear to my Father, if I never have to do another press conference, I'll die happy, come what may." Jess flipped through her note cards as she vented to Miranda, who'd made the short drive out to Gordon's, where Jessica's statement was to be made regarding her involvement in the assassination conspiracy.

When Wendy had asked her the night before where she thought would be a good location, Gordon's was the first place to pop into her head; she had enough happy memories there that she thought it might feel like home-field advantage, but without literally being at her home field again.

Also, she thought it might be nice to get a burger beforehand.

Destinee and Coach Rex slid into the booth across from where Jessica and Miranda sat, bringing with them the tray heaped with wrapped burgers, which they began to open.

The food smelled incredible as usual, but Jessica was horrified to discover that she wasn't hungry.

Is this what dying feels like?
YOU'LL FIND OUT EVENTUALLY.
Oh, look who's in a good mood today.
THE LORD HATH NOT MOODS.
We both know that's not true.
WELL, I'M NOT **MOODY**.
Must be nice. Benefit of being a man, I guess.
I AM NOT A MAN.
Oh. Well, male, I guess.
NOT THAT EITHER.
Wait. A woman? No way.
NO WAY INDEED.
Then what are you?
IT'S COMPLICATED.
Cool. I don't want to know.

Miranda waved to someone walking through the doors of Gordon's and Jessica, glancing up, spotted Chris. Instantly she felt that familiar glowing warmth that she got every time she saw his tan face and shiny blond hair, but then she remembered that she was furious with him. The sand bag in her stomach grew heavier.

"Sorry," Miranda whispered as he headed over. "I know y'all are fighting, but I figured you'd want him here."

Miranda was the only person Jessica had told about her argument with Chris, and even then it had only been the bare bones. Details about who said what and anything involving Mrs. Thomas were left out entirely since Jess wasn't even sure what *she* thought of all that yet.

Chris paused by the table, and Jess could feel his eyes on her head as she stared down at her note cards. "Can we talk?" he mumbled.

"Have a seat!" Destinee said, oblivious. "We probably have an extra burger somewhere in this pile. You can help yourself."

"Thanks, Mrs. McCloud, but I already ate." Chris refusing a burger was enough to tip off just about anyone that something was wrong, and Destinee was no exception.

"Everything okay?" she asked slowly.

Jessica sighed. "It's fine, Mom." She stood up and followed Chris outside the restaurant and around the corner where they could have some privacy.

"I'm sorry," Chris gushed as soon as they were alone. "I shouldn't have stormed into your house like that yesterday."

"I'm sorry I said all those stupid things."

"I wanted to apologize to you at lunch, but—"

She held up a hand. "I know." Or rather, she'd assumed he would try at some point throughout the school day. Only, after a late night of brainstorming, and considering a large portion of her classmates might be under the impression she was part of a conspiracy to murder everyone's favorite heartthrob (never mind that she was also the one who brought him back to life), it hadn't been a hard decision to take a sick day and stay home to practice her statement for that afternoon. Meaning poor Chris had no way to properly apologize all day.

"Are you okay?" he asked.

"Yeah, I'm fine. Just pissed."

He recoiled.

"No, not at you," she added. "At— I don't know. Everyone. Eugene Thornton. But it seems pointless to be mad at Eugene Thornton, because I'm always mad at him, and he keeps winning."

Chris took a step closer. He was only a foot away from where she leaned with her back against the brick exterior of the restaurant. "Except that time we made out in front of his news van when he wasn't expecting it."

Jessica chuckled, and the vibrations dislodged some of the dread clinging to the walls of her esophagus, allowing her to breathe more freely. "Yeah, that was good."

"Do you forgive me?" he asked, grinning mischievously.

She knew he was fishing, so she decided to tease him. "Yeah."

"Yeah? Just yeah? Cold, Jess."

She laughed. "Yeah, *I forgive you.*"

He closed his eyes briefly as the shiver crawled down his spine, then he leaned forward hesitantly, and when she tilted her mouth up toward his, he went for it.

Almost immediately after their lips connected, the wing beats of camera shutters exploded behind them.

Chris jerked back. "God dammit." He turned toward the source of the sound. A reporter Jessica had never seen before stood only a few feet away, camera held at chest level as the young, pale woman stood planted to the spot, seemingly terrified in the face of Chris's mild annoyance. Probably some amateur. There were more and more of those lately.

"Scram," he shot at the woman, who didn't look much

older than him and stood at least a foot shorter. The woman scrammed.

He turned back around. "Where were we?"

Jess frowned. "I need to get inside and go over my statement a couple more times."

He nodded understandingly and stepped away. "Hey, do you think your mom really meant it about y'all having an extra burger? I could go for a burger."

Jess sighed and grabbed his hand in hers. "Yeah, probably so." And they walked back inside.

Wendy had no time for burgers when she arrived fifteen minutes later, dressed in a tight skirt that emphasized her small waist and big hips, causing Chris's eyes to roam over her body when he didn't think Jessica would notice.

But Jessica noticed. Of course.

"I don't know that I can make myself any clearer," Wendy began once she'd squeezed into the booth next to Coach Rex, who didn't seem too put out by suddenly finding himself the meat of a Destinee and Wendy sandwich. "Read *verbatim* what's written on your cards. Don't worry about looking up from them. Don't worry about connecting with the audience. Just read the cards, and when you're done, say, 'Thank you, no questions, please,' which again, is written on the cards, so you shouldn't forget that, and then walk off the stage and head straight for Chris's truck, where he'll be waiting to get you the hell out of here."

"Can I say something?" Chris asked.

Wendy cocked a curious eyebrow at him. "Sure."

"You sound a little panicked."

Wendy laughed warmly, her voice like rolling ocean waves. "I don't get *panicked*."

"But you seem a little panicked."

Her nostrils flared almost imperceptibly. "I don't get panicked. I get intense. There's a difference."

He nodded. "Okay, fine." He pointed toward the tray at the center of the table, which had a single burger left. "Anyone have dibs on that?" Each person shook their heads. "Great."

As he grabbed it and dug in, Wendy stood. "Jess, we should get out there. Chris, you may want to eat that in your truck."

So it was happening. Jess sighed. Here went nothing.

She glanced out of the large windows overlooking the parking lot. The media was already waiting. Maria Flores and her camerawoman, Gabrielle, were set up, and when Jess locked eyes with the former, she waved and Jess waved back.

Wendy thought it best if they waited just out of sight until it was actually go time, but that meant Jessica's nerves had more opportunity to tie themselves in knots. She peeked out around the corner of the building to see which news teams had shown up on such short notice. Maria and Gabrielle from Channel Twenty-Four, the Channel Thirty-Six news team, who Jessica had gotten to know by name and face after three years of them being the last on every important story in her life. Spanky King was the sports correspondent for Channel Thirty-Six, but she supposed he'd managed to climb the ladder into the coveted position of Jessica correspondent as well. Good for him.

Two student reporters from the *Moremont Mundo* were there, too. Harris, a slightly jaundiced looking sophomore had spent the year trying to get an exclusive with Chris about Jessica—an interview Chris had refused time and time again on principle, since he'd once heard Harris mention that real men didn't feel the need to compete in sports to find self-worth. Along with Harris was the editor-in-chief of the newspaper, Stephanie Lee, who'd never personally pried into Jessica's life, but, Jess suspected, regularly sent others from the Mundo on reconnaissance missions to mine for dirt. Sneaky Stephanie. She wondered if the girl knew Chris had nearly run her over with his truck.

Then there were all the others, to whom Jessica had assigned nicknames to keep them straight. Sterling "Scrunchface" DiMaggio, Bret "Blue Eyes" Rosario, Latricia "Tight Lips" French, Monica "Big Britches" Fields—and those were just the local correspondents.

From out of town was Heath "Wink Monster" McGovern, Julie "Weasel" Chen, and "Stone Cold" Kevin Kelley. A handful of amateurs were there too, of course, but conspicuously absent from the bunch was Eugene "Punchable Face" Thornton. Did no one tell him about it? It seemed strange that he wouldn't have gotten word somehow, or if he *did* hear about it, that he wouldn't do whatever he could to be there for an easily twisted sound bite or sixteen.

Maybe he was dead. The thought brought a small smile to Jessica's worried face, but she knew better than to actually hope for that. Considering God shared a similar disdain for the reporter, it would be safe to assume Eugene's untimely (but not unwelcome) demise would be accompanied by an unexpected sun shower of butterscotch or perhaps a triple rainbow or maybe even an instantaneous mass extinction of mosquitoes.

But since none of that had happened, Eugene Thornton was very likely still kicking. *He just isn't here.*

That couldn't be good.

She shut her eyes. *Please don't let me or anyone I love get murdered by a sniper today.*

DON'T WORRY. NOT IN THE PLANS.

You're actually listening. Where's Eugene?

HE'S WITH JIMMY.

And what are they doing?

PLOTTING, OBVIOUSLY.

That doesn't sound good.

IT'S NOT.

"Ready?"

Jess opened her eyes and looked at Wendy. "Yes."

"Were you praying?"

"No. Well, actually. Yeah? I guess?"

Wendy nodded approvingly. "Great. Let's hope He answers your prayers." She guided Jess forward, out from the cover of the building, just as Jess replied with, "He did, but—"

Wendy leaned into her ear. "Smile on, but not too big. Read the cards, then split."

Jess sighed deeply and approached the microphones just as the avid crowd began to lose interest. It started with the

Wink Monster himself, who seemed to hear something in his ear piece that drew his attention away from the main attraction. When he glanced back up at Jess, whose focus was squarely on him, he tossed her a smile and a wink, like she was supposed to understand what in the hell *that* meant.

Next to lose focus was Scrunchface DiMaggio, whose face scrunched together in panic a moment before he turned his back to Jess and started hissing directions at his camerawoman.

Then the dominos began to fall, with Weasel, Tight Lips, Blue Eyes and Stone Cold becoming distracted, presumably by breaking news piping into their earpieces.

Something was happening.

It's Jimmy and Eugene.

Maybe because there was no question in her mind about it, God didn't bother responding. Or maybe he was preoccupied with Asia again.

She looked to the sky, didn't spot a triple rainbow or anything, really, other than a few clouds that had survived the heat of the day, and knew that it was too much to hope for.

Maria appeared by her side. "That *puto* beat us to it."

Was that Spanish for reporter? *Man, I should've paid more attention in class.*

"What's happening?" Wendy asked. For someone who said she didn't get panicked, she sure sounded panicked.

Maria listened to her ear bud for a moment, then said, "Here, follow me. Gabby has it cued up in the van."

It seemed that every van had it cued up, but Jessica

followed Maria Flores to hers. On the way, Destinee, Coach Rex, and Miranda intercepted them. "What's going on?" Destinee demanded.

"Not sure yet," Wendy said. "We're about to find out."

They huddled around the open door of the van, where Gabby had turned a large computer screen so that everyone could see it. There was a live stream on Eugene Thornton's news site.

For the moment, the shot was of Eugene standing in a place Jessica had visited only once, but she recognized the silver troughs behind him immediately.

"God dammit," Destinee breathed. Then much louder, "God *dammit!*"

SHE AIN'T LYING.

"Hush," said Wendy. "Can you turn that up at all?"

Gabby did, and they were able to make out what Eugene Thornton was saying into his microphone. "... And he's claiming that he has a major announcement that is totally unrelated to his mayoral race. Considering the setting he's chosen—the megachurch he founded over seventeen years ago—as the place at which he will make this announcement, we can only assume that this has *some* religious ties to the self-proclaimed Mooretown Messiah, better known in the White Light Church as the Embodiment of Original Sin, or simply the Antichrist."

"Oh boy," Jess mumbled.

Chris appeared behind her and placed his hands on her waist. "What's happening?"

"Watch," she said, pointing.

On the screen, the camera did a three-sixty to reveal

packed pews. How had Jimmy gotten so many people together without any other media besides Eugene Thornton knowing? Jimmy must have told them all not to tell anyone outside of the church.

Are all congregations so good at keeping secrets?

YOU KIDDING ME? CONGREGATIONS ARE THE BEST AT KEEPING BIG SECRETS. IT'S THE DAY-TO-DAY SECRETS YOU SHOULD NEVER TRUST THEM WITH. GOSSIP MONGERS.

Sort of the hog calling the mule dirty ...

Then Jessica spotted her. She was only visible in frame for a fraction of a second, but her face was unmistakable, seared into Jessica's mind like a nightmare: Mrs. Wurst.

And she was smiling.

Oh damn.

When the camera returned to Eugene, he said, "Looks like Reverend Dean is approaching the pulpit. Let's check in."

Jimmy was dressed in his Church Jimmy outfit, covered head to toe in white fabric that reflected the light streaming in through the long windows of the cavernous sanctuary. His signature red hog-hoof stole was draped around the back of his neck and down the front of his body. His slender face looked determined, his sculpted jaw set, and as a portion of Jess's brain still perked up at Jimmy's good looks each time she saw him, she'd learned just enough about chess in tenth grade and politics this year to know that she'd be facing checkmate as soon as Jimmy opened his mouth.

The room around him was already silent by the time he

reached his spot in the middle of the stage. He paused for a moment, feigning solemnity, but Jess had a feeling he was simply trying to prevent his glee from shining through.

"I'm coming to you today with an important confession," Jimmy said.

Even though (or maybe because) Jessica felt a delicate, quiet hope that Jimmy might come clean about everything, she felt fairly confident that whatever he was about to say would actually be *extra* unfortunate for her. Somehow. With Jimmy all things were possible.

"I have not been serving the Lord the way He has wanted me to these many years. The story I told you about young Jessica McCloud and my encounter with the Deus Aper was ... unfaithful to the truth in parts. Because the truth of it terrified me. The truth of it was much larger than I was prepared to face, and so I ran. But I'm done running, because God has visited me once more and He was a wrathful God, full of spite, rather than His usual somewhat apathetic disgust."

Did You—

NOPE. DIDN'T VISIT HIM.

"So, as I proceed onward in my humble pursuit of being the mayor of this great town, I find that I cannot move forward until I confess to all my loyal congregation.

"On that fateful night, seventeen years ago, God found me and led me to Destinee not only to show me that we are all pigs—"

"But God is Hog," replied the congregation out of habit.

Jimmy nodded. "But because the child that was born

that night wasn't the Antichrist, but in fact His daughter. The daughter of God himself, and the second Christ child."

The gasp from the crowd was drowned out by the gasps Jessica heard all around her, coming not only from the small group gathered at Maria's van, but those gathered at all the other vans, some of whom had their cameras pointed and rolling on their monitors, doing what they could to scrounge coverage of the *real* main event that day.

"Well I'll be damned," Destinee breathed from her place at the back of the group.

"No shit," said Chris.

Jess simply held her breath and waited for the other shoe to drop.

It didn't take long.

"God bestowed me with a purpose: to relay the message to Destinee and be His mouthpiece for all my years. As you can imagine, such a responsibility is enormous, and I fled like the little piggy I was, running wee-wee-wee all the way home.

"But I can no longer run. God visited me today wearing the flesh of another hog, and he explained to me in His merciful way, that without me, the Christ child's message cannot be heard, *will* not be heard. For He hath brought unto this world a daughter in a time when the voices of women are drowned out by the voices of men. And as a man, and God's chosen messenger, it is my duty to speak on behalf of His second child, the girl named Jessica McCloud, who henceforth shall be known as Jessica Christ."

Jessica's heart sank. Jimmy had come clean like she'd

always wanted. But he'd also stolen the narrative, *her* narrative, in the process.

And there was just no way she was down with being called Jessica Christ.

He wasn't done yet, though. "There was one who recognized this before me, one to whom I owe much of my revelation, outside of God's influence, obviously. And that is one of our oldest and truest members here at White Light Church, who was willing to tell the truth even if it meant being cast out of the church she loved. I speak, of course, of our own Ruth Wurst. Ruth, would you please stand?" Jimmy led off the applause and the camera rotated to frame up Mrs. Wurst, who clasped her hands in front of her and stared longingly at Jimmy.

It occurred to Jessica that Destinee now had another reason to beat Ruth Wurst's ass, and that she would very likely take it next chance she got.

She turned to see her mother's reaction to Mrs. Wurst's double-crossing only find *no one* standing in the place where Destinee had been only a moment before.

Her head swiveled around, trying to spot her mother in the crowd. Finally she did.

Destinee had already started the engine of Rex's Tacoma and was backing out of the parking spot over near the exit of Gordon's lot.

"Oh no." This couldn't be good. "Chris," she said.

"Are you hearing this?" he asked, not turning away from the screen.

"Chris!"

It wasn't just Chris who turned around this time.

Miranda, Wendy, Maria, Gabrielle, and Rex also stood staring at her. She pointed at Rex's truck as it pulled out onto the main road. "Uh, someone should stop her."

"What's she doing?" Maria asked.

Jess and Chris were already running for his truck, though, with Rex and Miranda not far behind.

"You don't think she'll do anything rash, do you?" Chris asked, as his truck lugged and chugged out of the parking lot and onto the main road.

"No," Jessica said from where she'd climbed into the front passenger's seat. "I *know* she'll do something rash."

"Like what?"

"Well, if we're lucky, she'll just beat Mrs. Wurst's ass for the third time."

"The *third* time?" Chris asked, blowing through a stop sign at an empty intersection.

"Yep."

"As mega hot as that sounds," Coach Rex spoke up from the back seat, "we can't let it happen. It'll all be caught on tape."

She's going to White Light, right?

YEP, AND MAN IS YOUR MOTHER HAULING THAT GLORIOUS ASS OF HERS.

"You need to step on it, Chris," she hollered.

"Bu-but, I'm a teen driver. I'll get us all killed."

Miranda huffed. "As much as I appreciate the concern, Chris, think about who's in the truck with you. We'll be fine. But if we don't catch Destinee before she single-handedly whoops every ass in that church, we'll be in even worse trouble. She might just whoop us too, if she's got enough momentum."

"Shit," breathed Chris. "I don't want to fight that woman."

"You absolutely don't," Jess agreed. "Trust me. She pulls hair."

She heard Coach Rex groan lustily from the back seat and wished she'd omitted that detail.

When Chris glanced in his rearview mirror, he sighed. "Looks like we got a tail."

Jess turned in her seat. Maria and Gabrielle followed in their van, and she could see Wendy's head sticking up between the two front seats.

"What do I do if we catch up to her?" Chris asked, taking a corner much too fast so that the occupants of the cab had to grab for whatever they could to hold on. "Do I ram her?"

"What the actual fuck?" Miranda said from the back seat.

"No, Chris, you don't ram my mother off the road!"

"I've never done this before!" he yelled defensively, his voice nearing a shriek. "I've never been in a high-speed chase! I don't know how this works."

"Neither have I," Miranda said, "but I still know you don't run a person you like off the road."

"Just stay behind her," Jessica said. "She's out of shape. One of us can catch her between the parking lot and the pulpit."

That plan only seemed to panic Chris even more. "I only scramble! You know I'm not a sprinter."

"It's true," Coach Rex corroborated from the backseat. "Best scrambler in the pocket in West Texas, but the boy can't keep up the speed over distance."

"I have a pretty decent 90-foot sprint," Miranda said. "Sometimes I can make it around first base and to second pretty quickly, but I'm not so great at the cuts."

Jess turned in her seat to look directly at her best friend. "Are you willing to tackle my mother?"

Miranda hesitated, then took a deep breath and nodded. "It has to be done. But you guys better not be far behind, because I don't want to have to struggle against her on my own."

"I'll be right behind you," Jessica said. "Just don't hesitate. You have to take her down. Whatever happens, we cannot let her beat the shit out of Mrs. Wurst, Jimmy Dean, Eugene Thornton, or anyone else at White Light. No matter how much we'd love to see it."

Jessica's heart fluttered dangerously in her chest. They needed to catch Destinee before she set a single foot inside the church. That was the only way they could avoid making the news.

Was a little bit of luck too much to ask for? Probably, but Jessica hoped for it anyway as the truck sped toward Midland.

Chapter Fifteen

They managed to catch up to Destinee about three miles before the Midland City Limits sign and about four miles before the massive billboard of Jimmy Dean's face that read, *Vote God back into this country. Reverend Jimmy Dean for mayor of Midland.*

Fortunately for those in Chris's truck, Destinee wasn't used to steering the Tacoma, and that slowed her down. But not by much. The Mooretown-to-Midland drive that usually took forty-five minutes had taken just under twenty.

The parking lot of White Light Church was still packed with the vehicles of those who'd turned up to see Jimmy's big announcement, which meant he was still bullshitting away. For a second, Jess was hopeful that it meant Destinee would be forced to park at the very back of the lot, making it easy for them to cut her off before she even made it through the goliath archway atop which the statue of Jimmy Dean had begun to gather grime in the crevices, but that was only because Jessica's thoughts were functioning under the assumption that Destinee gave a rat's ass about fire lanes.

Which, of course, she didn't.

The Tacoma came to a halt on the curb right by the front doors, and Chris had to slam on his brakes to keep from rear-ending her. The shock of the sudden stop caused a lag in reaction time and gave Destinee a head start as she left the front door of the truck wide open and took off at a dead sprint.

Had Jessica ever seen her mother run? She couldn't recall a time. Not even a jog. Destinee's form was awkward and flailing, but it didn't seem to slow her down.

Thankfully, Miranda didn't take her responsibility lightly, and she leapt out of the truck, already off on a dead sprint and almost to the front doors of the church before Jessica's feet had even landed on the sidewalk.

"Go, McCloud, go!" Coach Rex shouted from behind her.

Any chance of stopping Destinee before she made it inside had been immediately dashed the moment she'd parked Rex's truck in the fire zone and gotten the jump on them. So now it was a matter of not letting things go from bad to worse, and that proved enough motivation to keep Jessica's legs moving and arms pumping as fast as she could will them.

A tingling sensation began to spread out and intensify on her skin as she passed under the Arc de Jimmy and made it to the front steps, but she had more urgent things to focus on than a dumb, presumably heavenly phenomenon.

In the years between when Jessica had last entered through the perfectly Windex-ed glass front doors and the current moment, her memory had exaggerated the length of the aisle between the pews in the sanctuary to nearly a mile long. That's what it'd felt like the last time she was there, at least, fleeing from persecution by her mother's side.

But once she made it through the foyer and saw it again, she estimated it to be only about two-hundred feet long; not much further than from home plate to first then second base, if she understood those distances correctly (which she wasn't sure she did).

Destinee screamed incoherently as she tore down the aisle toward Jimmy, who seemed almost pleased to see her there.

Then Jessica realized what was happening, what had *been* happening, what would inevitably happen.

Shit. It's a trap.

But it's one I couldn't avoid. Checkmate.

She continued sprinting after Miranda, though, who was only a few feet behind Destinee as they rapidly closed the distance between them and the stage.

She glanced up at Jimmy where he stood. He didn't have a single drop of attention to spare for the rabid woman charging at him, spouting obscenities in between her strings of gibberish; he only had eyes for Jessica.

"Look who the Lord has brought us, as He promised me, and as I relayed to you only moments ago. How could I have known that Jessica Christ, of all people, would enter freely into this holy place, were it not something that God Himself had told me?"

Destinee slowed just for a second before she climbed the stairs on the side of the stage, and it was enough for Miranda to leap.

The image of a cheetah and gazelle popped into Jessica's mind, but she knew now wasn't the time for National Geographic, so she shoved it aside and caught up to the pair where they wrestled on the ground. She searched fruitlessly for an opportunity to jump in and help secure her mom so that Miranda didn't take a quick elbow to the chin.

Miranda took a quick elbow to the chin. She yelped and fell backward, and Destinee tried to get to her feet, but then Chris was there and he managed to hold her down in such a way that she couldn't get any leverage against him. A moment later, Rex jogged up, huffing and puffing, and tried to help Chris bring Destinee to her feet, but mostly he just clutched his heart.

Jessica tried not to think about how this would play out on Vine or Instagram or Snapchat or Twitter. Did Twitter do video? She'd have to check on that. Wendy would have a massive aneurysm when she saw it either way.

"Come here, sweet child. I beg your forgiveness as the Lord commands."

She glanced back at her mother, who seemed to be mostly subdued, and then sighed deeply. It looked like she had no choice but to try to confront Jimmy head on and see if she couldn't beat him at his own game.

Her expectations for such a positive outcome were not high.

She climbed the stairs onto the stage and Jimmy outstretched his arms.

Does he really think I'm going to hug him?

The idea was laughable. And yet … There was a part of her that was drawn to those open arms, a part that wanted to be embraced by him. Despite everything she knew about Jimmy, he still managed to be so damn huggable. How was that possible? Was it their history? Was it because she still, unfortunately enough, thought Jimmy was a little hot? Ugh. But screw that. He was a jerk. Jerks didn't deserve hugs.

When she denied him, he frowned and pouted exaggeratedly so that the camera could pick up the emotion clearly. Shitballs. Her impulse to hug him intensified.

FIGHT IT. RANDY WANTED A HUG, TOO.

But it's just a hug. It doesn't mean—

THOU SHALT NOT HUG THAT ASSHOLE.

Obviously I won't. But what do I do? How do I beat him?

YOU CANNOT. HE'S WON THIS ROUND.

What?!

SORRY.

Change it!

NOPE.

Please?

NOPE. HE'S WON. NOTHING SHORT OF A SMITING COULD—

Sounds good.

It's a Miracle!

THOU SHALT NOT SMITE JIMMY DEAN! I— HOW MANY TIMES DO I HAVE TO TELL YOU THIS?

"Look! See the way her face glazes over as she communes with the Lord? That was the same expression I wore when He spoke to me. Jessica"—she snapped out of it and looked at Jimmy, who'd given up on the hug thing, thankfully—"tell me what the Lord has said to you. Tell us all!"

"He called you an asshole," she said as loudly as she could, hoping the cameras picked it up clearly. Maybe Jimmy had won, but insulting him at least made her feel better.

Until Jimmy fell to his knees, clasped his hands in front of his chest, and stared up at the ceiling. "Oh Lord! You see all my sins, and You hath deemed me an asshole. I throw myself at the mercy of Your only begotten daughter, in hopes that You will work through her to forgive me."

He closed his eyes, bowed his head, and fell silent. Jess planted her feet where she stood. What the hell was Jimmy doing? Was he ... praying? No, surely that couldn't be right.

She glanced out over the pews, where each member of the church stared wide-eyed at the spectacle. They seemed to be holding their breath, and she wondered what sort of nonsense they'd been subjected to in the time between when she'd stopped watching in the news van to when she'd first sprinted from the foyer into the sanctuary.

This had to stop. If he'd already won, better to get it over with. She took a step forward, then another, until he was within arm's reach. She leaned down and extended her hand toward him, but before she made contact, his eyes shot open and he jumped up. She managed to control her bladder, which was full of Dr. Pepper from Gordon's, before she had a whole new situation on her hands.

"Yes, O Lord! I hear Your words," he shouted at the arched ceiling. Then he reached in his pocket and pulled out a small bottle of pale blue liquid. "Lord God has told me that it is now time for my cleansing." He held up the bottle. "One sip of this cyanide will be enough to kill me almost instantaneously, but the Lord hath commanded me to drink all of it to show my commitment and faith in Him and the miracles He works through his flesh and blood."

Is he really about to drink that?

YEP.

And how does drinking poison help him win? It seems like that would help him lose.

Jimmy tipped back the bottle, and she didn't try to stop him as it emptied down his throat and members of the congregation gasped and screamed. He recapped the bottle and slipped it back into the pocket of his white suit jacket.

Somewhere a child began crying.

"Now my life is in the Lord's hands. I shall approach the pearly gates and be judged. If He deems my repentance worthy of his mercy, He has promised to send me back through a miracle performed by his daughter. And I will return purified and ready to serve as her voice in a world that so desperately wants to reject the word of God through filthy sin. As I die a pig, may I humbly return, born again as a piglet."

Mrs. Wurst sat with her hands folded in the front row,

looking quite sure of herself, a serene smile on her lips as she nodded her head gently.

I wish I'd never brought her back.

OH FOR SURE.

Jimmy coughed then gagged before stumbling over to the pulpit to hold himself up as he began gasping for air.

A woman in the front row jumped up and screamed, "Someone help him!" But Jimmy looked up at her, his eyes becoming more bloodshot with each passing second of choking, and he held up a hand to stop her, even as he gasped and clutched at his throat.

"It's God's will," proclaimed Mrs. Wurst, and Jessica realized for the first time that Chief Wurst was not present. Neither were Courtney or Trent. Small blessings ...

She turned her attention back to Jimmy, who collapsed onto the velvety white carpeting of the stage. Horrible wrenching pushed its way up his windpipe in small bursts, and his face began to turn purple.

Jessica allowed herself the luxury of simply observing it. There wasn't anything she could do until he was dead anyway, so might as well enjoy the show.

A final perverse desire to hug him flowed through her body as his legs twitched one last time and then he was still. The silence was stifling. Even the sobbing from the audience had ceased.

As she looked out over the hundreds of faces in the pews and the hundreds more crowding into the back of the sanctuary, packed like sardines, she wondered if she'd be allowed to simply leave unharassed if she said, "Nah, I'm good," and refused to resurrect Jimmy.

The thought was tempting, oh so very tempting ...

Eugene Thornton's microphone hung dumbly in his fist, similarly to how his jaw hung dumbly open as he watched a man who Jessica could only assume he'd spent a significant amount of time plotting with lately, draw his last breath. Perhaps Jimmy was the closest thing Eugene had to a friend in Midland. That idea did nothing to *increase* Jessica's desire to resurrect the reverend.

"Do it, Jess!" yelled her mother from behind her.

Destinee was the last person Jessica would expect to hear that from. She turned to look at her mother, who then solved the mystery with, "If he stays dead, I don't get to whoop his ass!"

There was that. If watching her mother physically assault Jimmy wasn't on her bucket list before, now it was. High chance Chief Wurst would help dismiss the charges, too, even if this wasn't his jurisdiction.

Jessica knelt down next to Jimmy's unmoving corpse, leaning over him to inspect his purple face, which was starting to return to its normal golden tan.

He looked peaceful lying there, his eyes closed, voice shutting the hell up for once. If he was peaceful and his death made her life more peaceful, it didn't make much sense to change things.

Nope. She'd just leave his dead ass right where it was. There had to be a fire escape nearby she could make it to before anyone knew what had happened.

As the decision to let dead pigs lie began to take root in her brain, she reached down out of morbid curiosity, searching for a pulse. It was just good practice in the miracle biz, even if a resurrection wasn't going to be taking place.

She leaned forward, bringing her face closer to his as her fingers searched around for the jugular.

A small stream of air from his mouth flooded her nostrils with a minty-fresh scent.

What the—

And then her fingers found the jugular, and the pulse though his vein was hard and rapid.

I TOLD YOU HE'D WIN.

"God dammit, Jimmy," she hissed before he cracked open an eye and the corners of his lips twitched slightly.

He closed his eye again before gasping for air, drawing his knees up toward his chest and splaying his arms out from his side, clawing at the carpet.

"God ... dammit ..." Jess muttered again, as she stood up and backed away a few steps, giving him room to indulge in his theatrical thrashing as he pretended to convulse with God's mercy.

"Praise God!" came a man's voice from the crowd.

"Soo-ie!" called a woman.

Similar exclamations followed.

"It wasn't me," Jessica spoke into the mic on the podium. "I didn't do that. I didn't bring him back. He wasn't—"

Jimmy stumbled forward and shoved her to the side, looking worse for the wear, despite the whole thing being faked. He was really, really good at this.

"She tells the truth!" he said. "She didn't bring me back from the dead. God did! He worked through her because

He knew how much more I have to do on this earth before I'm allowed to enter the pearly gates, which He's assured me I'll be allowed to do, so long as I do not stray from the path He has laid out before me."

"It was mouthwash!" she shouted, but no one heard her words, which were drowned out by Jimmy's primal call to his people: "Soo-ieee!" and their divine Pavlovian response: "Soo-ieee!"

She turned her back on the reverend and walked toward the side of the stage, where Destinee, Miranda, Rex, and Chris waited patiently. She shrugged as she approached, saying, "What can ya do?"

Destinee looked too stupefied by the events that had just unfolded to even want to fight anymore.

"Why'd you just bring him back?" Chris asked, as she reached him and then walked past, down the stairs and around toward the aisle leading out of White Light. He and the others followed at her heels.

"I didn't. I decided bringing him back would be a stupid decision."

"Then what the hell happened?" Destinee asked from her left side.

Jessica fixed her eyes on the glass doors, knowing she could leave White Light Church today, but she wouldn't be rid of it for a long time, maybe not ever.

"Jimmy won. That's what happened."

The standing parishioners began pouring out of the pews, snorting and rushing the stage at Jimmy's beckoning. Seemed like another good call for Jimmy; him crowd surfing after supposedly being brought back from the dead by God Himself would go viral in no time.

Jessica shoved a young man who tried to push past her, sending him sprawling on the floor between an older couple, who stepped over him without hesitation.

"He can't win!" Destinee protested. "There's gotta be a next move for us."

"There is," Jessica tossed back over her shoulder. "We go home."

Chapter Sixteen

To get to Mr. Foster's office, Jessica had to pass by the trophy case at the front of the school. A third state championship football trophy had been added before the holidays.

If there was one upside to Jimmy Dean's victory over her narrative (and that was a huge *if*), it was that she'd been able to rejoin the football team again as the media fervor died down, losing interest in the daughter of God, preferring instead to go directly to the source, to God's mouthpiece, who had a much better way with words and who the camera loved.

A third state championship would have to be consolation enough for now.

Mr. Foster's door was closed as she approached his office after school. It was a big day, and not just because she'd had another awful week and finally, *finally* it was Friday. The day was notable because she'd made an important decision and she needed to tell the college counselor before she went and changed her mind again. After a year of meetings with him, which had mostly evolved into him leaning back in his chair, nodding and sighing along, while she informed him which college was the new top contender and usually discovered a new top contender by the end of it, she wondered what life would be like when she no longer had Mr. Foster to vacillate to.

She'd started to wonder things in a similar vein more and more frequently, now that the end of high school was so close.

What will like be like when I don't have to see any of the Wursts if I don't want to? She imagined it'd be great.

What will it be like to live in a big city? She imagined it would be like a dream come true to move around anonymously.

What will happen when Chris and I live in different cities? She imagined it would involve a lot less making out.

It was the last one that bothered her. She'd talked with her boyfriend earlier in the week, and he'd informed her solemnly that he had set his mind on Tech, knowing full well that she'd scratched that off her mental shortlist once she realized that Lubbock would be more of the same from Mooretown. And she knew that more of the same, with the exception of making out with Christopher Riley's face, just wasn't something she could take anymore of. The bottom line was that she didn't know if she could take another year in a small town. She'd heard rumors that the bigger the town, the less citizens gave a shit about one another, and while she usually heard it said like it was a bad thing, it sounded a little like Heaven to her.

So once it was settled that she wouldn't be in the same

town as Chris, her school selection could be based on other things. Things like whether or not she wanted to play college football, how far away from Mooretown she wanted to be, and whether hemorrhaging money for the next four years was worth living out of state.

The door to Mr. Foster's office opened, and Jessica jumped back when Courtney Wurst came flying out, a rare genuine smile on her face until she almost ran smack into Jessica, at which point she stopped in her tracks and the smile turned into the familiar sour-lemon face that Jess knew and loved so well. Courtney turned up her nose and walked by, clipping Jessica's shoulder with her own as she passed. *That* was a new behavior that had begun after Jimmy Dean's faked resurrection and was now a once-daily occurrence, if Jessica was lucky. If she *wasn't* lucky, which was mostly the case, she found herself shoulder checked an average of eight times a day by the Wurst daughter—before class, between each class and lunch, and then after school. It was clear the girl was going out of her way to find Jessica just to accost her.

The shoulder check outside Mr. Foster's office was number ten for the day—Courtney was in rare form heading into the weekend.

Surely her shoulder is as bruised as mine.

"Jessica, come on in."

She closed the door behind her to block out Courtney from her mind and entered into Mr. Foster's cozy room.

"I was just about to get started with the ritual throat-slitting of a goat. Care to join?"

"Ha-ha," she said sarcastically, trying not to laugh in earnest.

He beamed at her as she took a seat across from him. "Any big plans for the weekend?" he asked.

She had a feeling he genuinely liked her, which was quite a compliment, considering his overall feelings for humanity. It also left her with a peach pit of guilt in her stomach every time she remembered her conversation with Mrs. Thomas about how he was on his way out. Did he know yet? Would the right thing be to tell him so that he could at least start searching for another job?

But she wasn't here to discuss all that.

"Texas State."

His eyebrows pinched together as his brain attempted to piece together the non sequitur. "You're going to San Marcos this weekend?"

"No. Texas State. That's where I want to go. To college."

He nodded slowly and then a smile crept across his face. "That's a good school."

"It's four hours from Mooretown."

"Are you worried about the distance?" he asked.

"Yeah. I'm worried it's not far enough. But it'll do."

He laughed. "It'll more than do. Do you know what you want to study yet?"

She sighed. "No, not yet."

He folded his hands in his lap, still grinning approvingly. "Perfect. You'll fit right in there." After a moment's pause, he said, "So is that your *actual* decision, or do you intend to leave here one-hundred percent set on Michigan State?"

She'd omitted an important detail, one that, once she was firm on it, was the reason she chose Texas State over other, more distant (and expensive) colleges that were offering her a full-ride. "I don't want to play football."

He sat up straight in his chair. "Oh. Ohhh." He rubbed his hands together nervously. "Are you sure?" He cackled with laughter, then caught himself and regained his composure.

"Are you okay, Mr. Foster?"

He laughed again, this time more jubilant. "Yes, Jessica. I'm fine. I'm just … Never mind."

She couldn't tell if he was nervous, excited, or maybe both. Poor Mr. Foster. "Want to talk about it?" she asked.

He waved her off. "No, it's fine. Well, I mean—" He shut his mouth and thought about it, then reconsidered. "Yes. Yes, I would like to talk about it. No one's asked me. But since you're my last meeting of the week, and I think you might understand, sure. Well, it's a couple things. Mostly, I just met my quota."

"Your quota?" she asked.

"Yeah, for athletes versus non-athletes."

"So you had too many people going to college for sports?"

He nodded.

That seemed like a strange thing to care about. "Who says?"

He rocked his head back and forth. Was he not supposed to say? "Well, technically it's the nebulous 'leadership'"—he drew air quotes with his fingers—"but that just means Principal Thomas."

"Why wouldn't she want too many college athletes?"

He leaned over the desk. "Between you and me, I think she hates sports." He leaned back again. "But her stated reason is that she thinks it diminishes the academic accomplishments of the school if all the college-bound students we produce are on athletic scholarships."

"She doesn't hate athletics," Jessica said, feeling ... she couldn't put her finger on it. Torn? Confused? Icky? Yes, definitely icky.

Mr. Foster looked at her pityingly. "You've never been to a booster club meeting, have you?"

"No." Then, "Have *you*?"

He nodded. "Oddly enough, yes, I have. I was told it would be ... eye opening."

She didn't know what he meant by that or what about a stupid meeting where a bunch of parents sat around debating whose kid had better hand-eye coordination had to do with anything. What she did understand was that she didn't like what she sensed from Mr. Foster. He'd become her first line of defense and closest ally against bullshit, even if he was a little lazy or begrudging about his job from time to time, like Mrs. Thomas had mentioned. That was all easily overlooked and understandable, considering he worked in a school where all the adults seemed overtaxed, underpaid, and constantly one paycheck away from quitting, leaving it all behind, and pursuing whatever they were passionate about as children, money be damned.

But she wasn't sure that his hints of dislike for the principal were as excusable in her mind. And that was irritating. She didn't want to lose Mr. Foster as an ally. He was one of the few people in her life she was convinced *wasn't* the Devil.

"But don't *you* hate athletics, too?" she asked, grasping at straws.

He chuckled. "Hate? No. I actually used to play soccer in high school."

She tried not to roll her eyes. He *would* be a soccer player. They were a non-native breed to Mooremont High, which could never pull enough players to form a team, but she'd met a few at away games, and now that she thought about it, they were like young Mr. Fosters, with their lithe bodies and aloofness.

"If I'm being honest," Mr. Foster continued, "I'm just not the biggest fan of football. It stops and starts too much. There's no flow. But it doesn't matter what I think, obviously. If you wanted to play it in college, I'd support that, no matter *what* Mrs. Thomas not-so-subtly implied about my future job prospects, were that to have been your decision."

"Wait, what?" Did he know he was on the way out?

"Don't worry, though," he said. "I've been asked to leave a job for less. And between you and me, I'll probably not be asked back next year anyway, for some *other* dumb reason." But before she could ask anything else, he added, "So Texas State, eh? San Marcos *is* a beautiful city. Been dreaming about moving down there myself, actually. Seems to be everyone's pick today."

"Everyone's?"

"Well, not *everyone*, but you, and just a minute ago,

Courtney informed me she'd be going there, and before that—"

"The Wurst twins are going to Texas State?!" She hadn't meant to yell, but she probably couldn't have controlled herself if she'd had a second try at it, either.

Mr. Foster blinked dumbly against the outburst, then added, "No, not both. Just Courtney. Trent is going to Abilene Christian."

Now it was Jessica's turn to blink dumbly. "They're not going to the same school?"

He pressed his lips into an apathetic half frown and shook his head. "Nope. They're two separate people."

She had to let that sink in. *The Wurst twins are separate people.* They'd always seemed like two heads of the same dragon.

Mr. Foster started in on the process involved in officially accepting the offer of one university and rejecting the others, and when it became obvious that Jessica's mind was elsewhere, Mr. Foster interrupted himself with, "I'll email you all this and you can look over it this weekend. That work?"

She nodded and he opened his laptop and began working. "I should have your email on file, let me just check to make sure it's the one you want me to send it to." A few more clicks and he had it pulled up. "So it's mexicankicker7 at … Jesus Christ, Jessica, really? That seemed like a good idea?"

She shrugged. "At the time, yeah. I have a new one now, though. Wendy Peter— My PR rep made me get one."

He chuckled. "Well give me that one, then, and once you leave here today, give Wendy a raise and maybe a thank-you card from me."

Chapter Seventeen

Jessica waited until the very last second to wipe off the excessive makeup that Destiree had insisted was appropriate for senior prom and wondered if her mother had ever made it to prom herself. Considering Jessica was a toddler at the time, probably not.

The lipstick had felt like butter, and the dark eye shadow made her eyes look sunken. Chris would be too nice to say anything about it, but she knew that all the primping really wasn't necessary; he'd smelled her at her worst for three football seasons and he was still with her. As long as she didn't smell like ass—and she was as sure as one can be that she didn't—everything would be okay.

That didn't make her any less nervous, though. Not only was this prom night, the lead-up to which had been full of nothing but sexual innuendos bordering on accusations from the football team, but tonight was also the night Jessica decided to let down Chris by telling him where she'd decided to go for college, knowing full well he would be going somewhere else. She'd been sitting on the decision for a week, and she couldn't hold out any longer. Breaking the news on a big night like this, with so much else going on, seemed like an easy way to slip it in without it becoming a huge thing.

Jessica waited in her room for the sound of the F-350, and checked her Twitter as a nervous tic. She'd tweeted earlier that day, *Finally decided on a university. More info soon.* It was her warm-up for breaking the news to a smaller and more important audience of one, and so far she'd received three hundred and ninety-four notifications on that alone. Wendy had told her to respond to as many as she could—steady followings were built one relationship at a time.

Chris arrived in her driveway just after she rolled her eyes at one of her follower's jokes but replied with *@Jscacrst69 lol* anyway, and she slipped her phone into the clutch that matched her emerald green dress, adjusted the straps on the wedges she could hardly walk in, despite ample practice, and headed out into the living room where Coach Rex and Destinee were waiting.

The way they looked at her, all toothy grins and pride, was mortifying. "I can't wait to take this stupid dress off," she mumbled, feeling a blush creep onto her cheeks.

"I bet Chris can't wait for that, either."

It was Coach Rex who said it, and six months ago, Jessica would have been surprised to hear him say something so ribald, but clearly her mother's influence had gotten to him.

Destinee cackled and clung to his arm, and Jess hoped that they'd have worn themselves out by the time she made it home after prom; a night off from hearing the hammering of Destinee's bedpost against the wall would be a real blessing, if she believed in such things. But she knew better. If God could have stopped Destinee from engaging in night aerobics with Rex without some terrible consequence resulting from the divine intervention, He already would have.

"Speaking of which," Destinee said, "you didn't take out the condoms I put in there, did you?" She nodded at the clutch in Jess's hand, which Jessica then opened.

"You mean these?" She pulled out the long string of condoms, all twenty-four. The packaging never stopped reminding her of the long strings of lollipops she'd always asked for at the store but which Destinee had claimed would rot her teeth out. So instead, Jessica got condoms. "I already told you I'm not going to need one, let alone two dozen."

"And I already told you if you use one, you'll use two dozen. That boy's been dating you for over two years now, and you still haven't given him the goodies? If you think your first time won't be immediately followed by your second, third and eventually twenty-fourth time, you got a lot to learn, baby."

Chris knocked on the door and Jessica hurriedly shoved the condoms back into her clutch and pinched it shut.

She opened the door, feeling relieved that it was finally time to get going and get this awful rite of passage over with.

But when she caught sight of Chris, her blood pressure

shot up like she'd just run ten suicides with no break in between.

Holy shit, he looked good.

"Damn," said Destinee from behind her, and Jess couldn't help but agree.

What child support money he hadn't spent on Gordon's burgers over the years, Chris had put into a savings account, which he never dipped into, with the exception of the tux he now wore with an emerald green bowtie to match her gown. Part of her had expected him to look silly all dressed to the nines, like how she felt herself, but he looked natural in the tailored jacket that accentuated the broadness of his shoulders, cutting in to his trim, muscular waist.

He smiled and took her in, eyeing her from head to toe then back up again, pausing at the small bit of cleavage she'd mustered, then back to her face. "You look beautiful, Jess."

"You look like a spy."

He grinned. "Thanks."

"Pictures!" Destinee proclaimed, and Jessica groaned.

Chris leaned in close so only she could hear. "Gives me an excuse to put my hands on your body."

She snorted and felt her face redden again but became much more at peace with the awkwardness of standing in the run-down McCloud home until her mother was satisfied that she *must* have a good picture by that point. "If not," Destinee added, "I'll just Photoshop it."

Destinee had no knowledge of or access to Photoshop, but Jessica nodded along like it was a viable option, and then scooted Chris out the door and to his truck. He opened the passenger-side door for her, but before she got in, he closed the space between them and kissed her roughly. When he pulled back, he said, "I have reservations at Gordon's for seven. We should get going."

"You have ... wait, what?" She climbed into the truck and he shut the door carefully behind her before circling around to the other side. She must not have heard that correctly. He must have meant somewhere nicer, like Texas Roadhouse or Chili's.

Once he was back inside and started up the engine, she debated whether or not to ask him for clarification. On the one hand, she did love Gordon's, and she didn't want to make him feel bad about botching prom-night dinner plans. But on the other hand, what the hell?

She decided to just wait it out. Surely he'd *meant* another restaurant, but just had Gordon's on the brain, like always.

She held onto that hope until they finally pulled into the parking lot of Gordon's, at which point, she was forced to accept that, yes, Chris was taking her to a fast-food burger joint for prom dinner.

Once the initial shock of that wore off, she realized something else. "Are they even open?" The parking lot was empty, but there were dim lights on inside, and she thought she saw Jeremiah, the general manager, standing behind the counter.

"Yep, they're open," he said, sounding almost giddy.

He parked on the curb right in front of the doors and went around to let her out, helping her down so she didn't break an ankle trying to climb out in her wedges. "Uhh." Her brain still couldn't make sense of it as he opened the first set of glass double doors. "Where is everyone? What's going on?"

"I told you," he said, holding open the second set of doors, "I made a reservation."

She paused as she entered and was finally able to process the surroundings. Strings of icicle lights dipped here and there across the ceiling, replacing the usual fluorescent lighting, and in the booth where they usually sat were three long, lit candles. "You reserved the whole place?" she asked dumbly, already knowing the answer was "No shit," but feeling the need to ask anyway.

"Yep," he said proudly, and then he offered the crook of his arm. She paused before taking it and looked up at him. He was quite impressed with himself. Okay then.

She pushed the weirdness factor of the grand gesture to the back of her mind and took his arm, and he led her straight over to the booth.

"Shouldn't we order?" she asked.

He looked down at her, his eyebrows scrunching together. "Oh," he said after a second. "You're serious. No. We don't need to order. I—we're the only ones here. I already have that all sorted out."

"Ah, okay. Yeah, that makes sense."

She slid into the booth, careful not to snag her dress on the cracked vinyl, and he scooted in across from her.

The large candles glowed between them, and a second later, Jeremiah brought over two wine glasses, set one in front of each of them, and then began pouring them Dr.

Pepper from a one-liter bottle that he had wrapped a clean dish towel around.

That was the last straw before Jess started giggling. She couldn't stop. She tried, and for a second she thought she'd manage it, but when she looked up at Chris and he started laughing, she was done for. She laughed until she snorted, and then she laughed harder, until tears began to form in her eyes and she worried that if she didn't stop soon, her stupid mascara would become a problem. Vanity was just the thing she needed to calm herself down, and as she relaxed, she looked up at Chris. "I needed that," she said. "This is amazing."

He was still giggling. "Yeah, this is ridiculous. It seemed a lot more romantic when I came up with it."

"And when was that?"

"Last week. While I was eating a burger here."

That set off the laughing again, and once they were both able to control themselves, Jess knew that fun time was over, and she needed to just come out with her bad news. She'd miss in-person moments like this with Chris, once they were in a long-distance relationship, but it'd be worth staying together if they were able to meet up for burgers every so often. She wondered what town was halfway between Lubbock and San Marcos. She'd have to look it up next chance she got.

"Chris, we need to talk, and don't worry, I'm not breaking up with you."

He nodded determinedly. "Okay, that's good. I've been meaning to tell you something, too."

The sudden seriousness of his voice caused her hackles to bristle. "Wait, what?"

"I didn't want to talk about it tonight, because I didn't want to ruin anything, so maybe we can just wait until tomorrow."

"Like hell," she said, wishing she didn't sound so much like her mother every time she felt threatened.

He sighed. "Yeah, okay. Might as well get it out."

But before either of them could say what was on their minds, Jeremiah approached the table, setting down a plated burger and fries for each. Jessica's was the usual double with extra cheese, no mustard that she ordered each time she came, and Chris's was what had jokingly become known as the Rowdy Riley and consisted of four patties stacked with a slice of cheese on top of every one. It was served with a small dish of ketchup, which was what he dipped portions into before taking each bite.

But he didn't immediately dig in like he usually would. Instead, he thanked Jeremiah who nodded and then headed back into the kitchen, leaving them with the tough decision to talk or eat.

Chris made the call. "I'm not going to Tech," he said. "I should have told you sooner, and I feel bad, because I know you said you'd think about it so we could go to school together, but I changed at the last second and forgot to tell you, and now it's probably too late because you've already accepted at Tech. But I want you to know I'm okay with the idea of a long-distance relationship, so—"

"Wait." She held up a hand to stop him. "Where are you going instead?"

"They offered me a full ride and my odds of becoming the starting QB by sophomore year looked more promising."

"Okay, fine. That's great. But where are you going?"

He paused and took a deep breath. "Texas State."

She chuckled. "No shit."

He looked like he was going to be sick. "Jessica. I promise, we can make it work. I want to make it work."

"Well no shit we can make it work," she said. "I'm going to Texas State, too."

He tucked in his chin and arched an eyebrow at her. "Huh? But I thought—"

"Nope. I changed last minute, too."

"Really? But I thought you didn't want to live on a fault line."

She shrugged. "God promised me it was inactive."

Chris nodded and when he flattened his burger with the palm of his hand before taking his first bite, she knew he was just trying to buy himself some time to reassess everything.

She started on her burger, despite the restriction of the dress around her middle.

Chris swallowed his first large bite. "So we're going to Texas State together."

Jess nodded. "I guess so."

"That's awesome."

"Yeah, it is."

As she took another bite of her burger, he just happened to mention, "I love you."

She choked, but managed not to die, which was good,

she supposed. She crammed the unchewed piece into her cheek. "What?"

"I love you." He waited patiently, wearing the same determined look she'd seen on him before each state championship.

Her mouth was hanging open. She should do something about that. She shut it. "I ..." She took a deep breath. "I love you, too."

Chris's intensity deflated and he let his breath out in a whoosh. Saying it back was the right choice—she knew that instantly. Two and a half years of dancing around it was long enough. Now she just had to decide if she really meant it. And what it really meant.

It did lighten the mood a bit, like a burden had been lifted off both of them, and Chris was able to dive into the story of how he'd managed to convince, or more aptly *guilt*, Jeremiah into letting him reserve the restaurant for a full hour on a Saturday night. Jessica laughed along at Chris's wild gesturing, and when the hour was finally up, she wished he'd managed to drag out the reservation longer, because now came the event she'd been dreading for months, ever since it first occurred to her that she would have to attend it.

Now came senior prom.

* * *

The plan had been to arrive fashionably late to prom so they weren't the first ones there. Their reservation at Gordon's ended thirty minutes after the dance was supposed to begin, so Jess felt good about the timing. The gym would already be packed, and the two of them could slip in unnoticed without incident. But when they pulled into the Mooremont parking lot and were able to find parking in the first two rows, Jessica felt less confident.

"It was supposed to start at 7:30, right?" she asked.

Chris nodded. "Yeah, I thought so."

"Where is everybody?"

He shrugged. "Fashionably late? You want to wait until more people show up?"

She looked around at the other cars and spotted Miranda's. "No, I don't want to leave Miranda hanging. Hard enough going stag to prom, but to have to sit around with almost no one else must be unbearable."

Jessica's assumptions were proven wrong on two accounts once she entered the gym that had been redecorated to feel like a Caribbean beach. (Or what teenagers who've never seen a Caribbean beach assume one would look like. The fake grass and inflatable palm trees weren't exactly romantic. Neither were the LED tiki torches that lined the walls or the coconut shell candy dishes along the refreshment table.)

Jessica's first wrong assumption was that few cars in the parking lot meant few people inside. As it turned out, the majority of her classmates were already there, dancing with their dates, some of whom she recognized, some of whom must have been from neighboring towns. It made sense, she supposed, that most of them wouldn't have driven themselves, considering how many had spent the past month talking about how hammered they planned on being for the event.

The second wrong assumption was that Miranda would be alone and possibly feeling sorry for herself for not having a date to prom. Jess realized she was off on that account as soon as she glimpsed Miranda through a dense forest of male classmates that congregated around her as she regaled them with a story that Jess could only guess at.

When Miranda spotted Jessica and Chris, she paused in her animated storytelling and pushed her way through her mentourage to run over to greet them.

The wispy powerhouse of a pitcher looked like a classic Hollywood starlet with her silky, form-fitting light blue ankle-length dress, the sides of her white-blonde hair swept back into a barrette to fall in long tendrils down her back. Jessica had never seen Miranda in makeup, but she wore it well—much better than Jessica, who'd felt like a clown the instant she'd seen herself in the mirror. With the exception of Miranda's shimmery eye shadow, it didn't even look like she was wearing makeup; it just looked like she was extremely pretty.

"Hey! How was dinner?"

"Hey ... good," Jess replied automatically as she leaned forward to hug her best friend.

When Miranda pulled back and then stepped toward Chris, Jessica felt something twist in her gut just before he leaned forward and gave her a hug.

He pulled back and looked approvingly at Miranda. "You look pretty."

Another twist. Maybe the Gordon's wasn't sitting well.

"Thanks! And you look handsome. Like James Bond or something," Miranda added cheerily.

"That's what I said," Jessica interjected.

Chris tilted his head to the side. "Well, you said I looked like a spy."

"Same thing."

"Not the same."

Miranda's eyes darted back and forth between Jess and Chris. "Uh ... they have good punch. I'm fairly certain it's not spiked. Or not with anything that has a taste."

"Good enough for me," Chris said. "Lead the way."

By the time nine o'clock rolled around, there was almost no space to move in the packed gym. The bass rattled in Jessica's chest as she looked around the room and wondered if she'd miss these people or if, on the whole, she'd be glad to leave. They were all she'd ever known, after all. Maybe this was a good as it got? Maybe she wouldn't understand how much they meant to her until she could no longer see them every day.

She danced with Chris on the slow songs, but neither were particularly keen on grinding, so when the music sped up, they took a break to stand on the edge of the gyrating crowd, holding hands. Jessica was torn between telling Miranda that they'd finally said, *I love you* or taking that tidbit to the grave with her. Even just thinking about it created a hot buzzing in her brain and left her feeling inexplicably embarrassed.

When the third fast song in a row began to play, Chris leaned close and said, "Follow me," and then led her through the crowd and to the doors leading to the hallway.

Chris went to open it, but a freshman teacher, who had spent the evening looking less than thrilled at being here on a Saturday night, stepped in front of him. "No one in and out," she said.

"It's just for a second. I just forgot something in my truck."

The teacher rolled her eyes. "Sure. You and everyone else."

The door opened suddenly in front of them, and Jess jumped back, startled. Mrs. Thomas appeared in the doorway, beaming amicably at Jess, as usual. "Oh, look who it is! Don't you two look lovely?"

"Thanks," Jess said. Chris stayed silent.

"Coming out?" asked Principal Thomas, pulling the door wider and holding it for them.

"Yeah," said Chris. Then he added, "Just forgot something in the truck."

Mrs. Thomas waved him off. "No worries. Hurry back. They're announcing the prom king and queen in a few." She winked conspiratorially, and Jessica and Chris moved past her before she entered into the gym and the door closed behind her, shutting out the noise.

"You don't think ..." Jess began, afraid to even vocalize her suspicion. Part of her wanted it to happen, but part of her knew it wouldn't work out well for her.

"What, prom king and queen? Us?"

She nodded.

"Uh, yeah. It's a shoo-in."

"Damn."

It's a Miracle!

"Nah, it won't be so bad." He led her down the hallway away from the parking lot.

"Wait, where are we going?"

It was only a short walk before she found out.

"He fixed the lock at the start of last year, though," she said.

Chris reached into his tux and pulled out a key. "Yep. And he gave this to me yesterday." He turned and unlocked the door to Coach Rex's office.

So Chris and Rex had plotted behind her back. She stepped in and he closed the door behind her, locking it. "I thought it might be fun to make out where we first kissed."

Chris was on his game tonight, that was for sure. She turned toward him, fingering her clutch nervously, but when her eyes locked onto his, the nervousness melted away.

Good God, he was hot. At some point in the past few months, he'd started to look like a man. And the tux helped.

He grabbed the clutch from her and tossed it to the side. It landed on the cement floor a split second before he grabbed her and pulled her in, pressing his lips to hers, reminding her for the millionth time that he was unbelievably well-endowed as he pressed said endowment against her stomach.

Except this time it didn't scare her.

She felt her stomach tighten, sure, but it was in a different way than before.

Yes! She felt her heart flutter in her chest. *Yes! Yes! Yes! Hell yes!* The realization made her feel suddenly light-headed, but luckily she was able to relax and let Chris's strong arms keep her on her feet.

He broke the kiss and looked down into her eyes. "God damn, Jess, all I've been able to think about all week is—" Something caught his attention, and he turned his head toward it. It was something on the ground. "That," he said.

Jess turned to see what it was.

The impact had caused her overstuffed clutch to pop open, and the roll of condoms dangled out.

She looked back at him. While he didn't seem put out, he did seem surprised. "Goddamn, Jess. I mean, I guess we're on the same page, but ... goddamn. You don't mess around."

She grimaced. "Better safe than sorry?"

He laughed and then bit his lip. "Damn, Jess. I want to take you in the back of my truck right now"—she understood that was intended to be romantic—"but we need to go knock out the prom stuff first. Then..." He let the insinuation hang in the air, and she understood that, too.

Then they would lose their virginity together.

The plan sounded like a good one. It finally sounded like a good one.

Praise whoever!

When they headed back into the gym, Miranda was slow-dancing with Lewis Walker, yet another reminder that Jessica hadn't upheld her duties as best friend the way she should. Last she'd heard, Miranda still hated Lewis. Had they gotten back together?

Emma and Sandra walked onto the small stage where the DJ had set up, and after flipping their stiff, styled hair an absurd amount of times and flashing toothy grins and pretending they didn't even realize they were on stage and everyone was looking at them, the DJ paused the music and handed them a microphone, which Emma held while Sandra held Emma's wrist to keep the microphone where she could also speak through it.

"Okay everyone," Emma said. "As president"—she pointed at herself—"and vice president"—she gestured vaguely at Sandra—"of the senior class, we have a very important announcement to make. The ballots are tallied, and we're ready to announce the prom king and queen of Mooremont!" Emma led the clapping, slapping her hand against the microphone, causing thuds to blast out from the speakers. The DJ shut his eyes to brace against the equipment abuse.

"But first, the *other* members of the court," Sandra said. She looked out into the crowd and shielded her eyes. "Mom?" she said, not into the microphone.

Mrs. Thomas came scurrying up to the stage, a stack of envelopes in her hand, which she waved above her head. "Official results!" she said, and handed the envelopes to her daughter.

"Principal Thomas counted these herself," Emma explained, "because *some people* seemed concerned that the results might not be accurate otherwise." Her eyes fell specifically on one person in the crowd, though from where Jessica and Chris stood by the refreshment table, it was hard to tell who had apparently called into question Emma's (no doubt questionable) integrity.

Sandra grabbed Emma's wrist again and pulled the mic

to her mouth. "The duke and duchess are the boy and girl who received the third most votes for prom king and queen. This year's duke is …" She drew out the suspense as she opened the envelope and pulled out the result, but Jess knew for a fact no one wanted to be anything other than King or Queen. Duke was a consolation gift that was more embarrassing to win than not winning anything. "Trent Wurst!" Sandra announced it like anyone would want to hear it.

But Trent seemed to consider it validation enough, and he strutted onto the stage to receive his sash, which Emma grabbed from the table behind her and threw over his shoulder. Subdued clapping welcomed him into the annals of Mooremont High history.

Sandra began on the second envelope. "And this year's duchess is …" She pulled out the results and grinned, presumably because it wasn't her. "Courtney Wurst!"

Jess was unable to stifle her laugh, but that was okay, because it was drowned out by the awkward laughter of everyone else in the gym. Once Courtney had received her sash, she stood on stage next to her twin, both their arms folded across their chests. His sister's award seemed to have tainted his, and Jess wondered for the first time if maybe the Wurst twins hated one another.

"Okay!" said Sandra. "And now moving on to the prince and princess!"

"Or as they say in Italy, the *principe* and *principessa*," added Emma, who had spent spring break in Rome with her family and was now apparently an honorary Italian.

Sandra opened another envelope. "And the prince is …"

She pulled out the note and Jessica could spot her distaste, even from this distance. "Greg Burns?"

Jess knew she'd spotted Greg in the gym earlier, but no one approached the stage. The other seniors started to get antsy and look around, including Emma and Sandra. Then Emma pointed to someone. "Greg. Get up here."

Greg took his time coming onto the stage, and Jess suspected he was high as a kite as Emma slipped a small crown onto his head and herded him to the side of the stage by Courtney.

"The princess," Sandra said, clearly wanting to move on, "is ..."

Jessica shut her eyes. *Please not me, please not me ...*

"Emma Sanderson!"

Emma pretended to be excited, though it was obvious she'd been hoping for queen. She'd certainly been campaigning hard enough for it.

She scurried over to the table and popped on the princess tiara before plastering a smile on her face.

"Okay, and now for the big stuff! This year's prom king and queen!"

The crowd seemed excited enough, clapping, some whooping, a male classmate shouting the obligatory, "Take it off!" at the temporary emcees.

Sandra opened the envelope as she breathed deeply. "This year's prom king is ..." She pulled it out and said quickly, "Chris Riley."

Chris leaned down and kissed Jessica quickly. "Told ya," he said before cutting his way through the crowd and hopping on stage to receive his crown and scepter.

Seeing him up there, waiting for a queen, Jess realized that she actually *did* want to win that title, so she could stand next to him and get a little glory. It would also mean that her classmates didn't all actively hate her like she suspected.

But Sandra still hadn't received any honorary titles yet, and it seemed unlikely that the entire class would overlook her. Jessica tried not to think too hard about the smug look on Sandra's face if she got to be Jessica's boyfriend's queen.

Sandra seemed to think it likely, at least, as she took her time coyly opening the envelope and said, "And this year's prom queen is ..."

Please don't let it be Sandra, please don't let it be Sandra ...

Sandra slipped the paper out slowly, and when her eyes fell on it, she scrunched her brows together in a look that was a mixture of disappointment and confusion.

"Miranda Forte?"

The crowd didn't seem at all confused about it, and applauded enthusiastically, especially the men who'd been swarming her all night.

Was Miranda popular?

She'd never considered the question before. She'd just assumed that because most people avoided *her*, they'd avoid her best friend, too. But maybe that wasn't the case. Maybe Miranda hadn't been sitting home alone every night she wasn't with Jess. Maybe while Jessica was spending time with Chris, Miranda was out cultivating a healthy social life.

And sure, she'd led the softball team to a state championship this year, but Jessica had done that with football, and for the past three years. That alone didn't make a person popular, clearly.

At least it's not Sandra, she told herself, but as Miranda received her crown and scepter and went to stand beside Chris, Jessica struggled to repress the thoughts that were trying to seep out from the darker parts of her mind. Chris and Miranda hugged and the photographer began taking frantic pictures of the court.

"Wait," Sandra said suddenly. "We're not quite done yet."

Some of the chaos died down, and Jessica held her breath.

"The class officers decided that there was one more award that we just had to give away, one that *we* would decide among ourselves ...

"Our time at Mooremont had its defining moments and its memorable characters, but there was one person who was *extra* memorable."

Oh shitballs.

Emma nodded and took it from there. "And so we wanted to make sure that she was recognized for her overall contribution to school spirit."

Those closest in proximity to Jessica were starting to catch on, and looked over at her for a reaction. She hoped it wasn't obvious how hard she was clenching her jaw.

"Her impact on keeping all of this senior class constantly entertained has, let's just say, been *huge*." Emma grinned mischievously into the crowd. "So we thought, well who keeps the spirits of the court high? Duh! The jester! So Mooretown High's first ever prom jester goes to —you guessed it—Jessica McCloud!"

Jessica glanced up at the stage, where Chris and Miranda stood in their regalia, both of their mouths lolling open at this new sadistic trick Emma and Sandra had devised and no doubt subsequently spearheaded.

I don't have to go up there if I don't want to.

Emma pointed directly at her in the crowd. "Come on, Jess!" She said it like this wasn't cruel and unusual punishment.

The image of Jimmy beckoning to her with open arms flashed in Jessica's mind so vividly, he might as well have been standing on stage between Emma and Sandra.

I don't have to go up there and I'm not going to go up there.

But then someone gave her a shove in the back, causing her to stumble forward.

Oh hell, I'm already moving in this direction, maybe it would be easier to just get it over with and then get out of here and get laid.

She took one step forward but stopped again when Chris shook his head slowly but firmly and Miranda mouthed, *Nooooo*.

"Come on!" Emma insisted again. "We all know you don't mind being the center of attention."

Jess tried to breathe through the hot pressure that was building behind her eyes and sternum.

She needed to leave. That force gathering in her body was begging to tug free, and the last thing she wanted was to accidentally injure or kill people who didn't deserve it.

She turned and tried to head toward the doors, but the crowd wouldn't move out of her way. She tried to elbow through, but an arm reached out and blocked her path. She looked up at the face associated with the arm and saw Drew Fenster staring at her.

This fucking guy.

An inflatable palm tree popped to her left and those in the crowd closet to it screamed. Several students dropped to the floor.

"Not a gun, just the palm tree!" Sandra hollered over the mic, and attention refocused on Jessica. "Come on, McCloud! Everybody's waiting for their favorite clown!"

"Move," she growled at Drew.

He scoffed at her.

A row of the LED tiki torches exploded, one right after the other and Drew had the sense to step aside.

But another kid—one she didn't recognize and therefore had to be from another school—stepped in Jessica's way.

"*Move!*" she said, shoving him.

He stumbled back, but regained his feet and stood his ground again, chuckling in alarm and amusement. If only she had a big, strong date who could knock this guy to the floor ...

She looked up at the stage to see when Chris would get with it, but her attention shifted to Greg almost immediately when he shouted, "Stop throwing a tantrum and just get your damn hat so we can get out of here. Fuck, Jess."

"God dammit, Greg!" she shouted.

The wrath tugged free and the rest of the tiki torches blew. Next went one of the goliath hanging gym lights, and the screams that followed as students fled from the glass raining down from above were temporary drowned out by the deafening screech of feedback from the DJ's sound system. Emma dropped the mic and covered her ears and the last thing Jessica saw before she smote the rest of the overhead lights into twinkling falling shards was Chris taking three purposeful steps across the stage, rearing back and decking Greg straight in the temple.

During the span of seconds between when darkness swallowed the gym and when the emergency lights blinked on, blanketing the panicked crowd with a red glow, it was all Jessica could do to avoid being shoved over and trampled.

However, she did feel slightly less angry, but she wasn't sure if that was because she'd opened up the smiting pressure valve or because she had just witnessed Greg getting punched in the head. She could sort out the particulars later, she supposed.

An arm wrapped around her waist and she knew on instinct that it was Chris.

"Let's get out of here," he hollered over his shoulder as he cleared a path through the crowd the way she'd seen his offensive line do for him a hundred times on quarterback sneaks.

"Wait, where's Miranda?" She pulled against him until he stopped his progress.

"Right here," said a voice from behind her.

Jessica whipped her head around and spotted her best friend, who appeared remarkably calm. They grabbed hands and Chris led them the rest of the way through the crowd and out an emergency exit, which seemed appropriate, considering.

It's a Miracle!

The calmness of the night air felt irreverent by contrast. Jess turned to check on Miranda. "You okay?"

"Of course," she said. "I know you wouldn't smite me."

Jessica stole one last glance into the gym, where her classmates were still scrambling for the main exit, all consideration for the safety of others forgotten.

Good. Let them panic.

The emergency door shut slowly, and as it did, Jess knew for a fact that she wouldn't miss Mooremont High. Not even a little.

Chapter Eighteen

Jessica only knew this spot from having been here once with Chris more than two years ago. It was where they'd shared their first real kiss ... before being interrupted by a cock-blocking mission from God.

While Jess had started the night on the fence about sex, Chris was another story entirely. It was clearly no split-second decision to bring her out here—the solar-powered paper lanterns set up around the clearing just off the dusty farm-to-market road was what tipped her off to this being highly pre-meditated—and she wondered if he had a plan B set up in another part of town, in case she'd said she wanted to continue waiting, which would have been entirely understandable given the unfortunate, smite-filled turn prom night had taken less than an hour before. Or maybe he'd have brought her here anyway to sweeten the pot and hopefully convince her that now was the time.

A freeing sense of Nihilism had settled on Jessica's mind between when she and Chris parted with Miranda to

It's a Miracle!

hurry to his truck for a quick getaway and when they arrived in this special spot, and perhaps the only thing in this world that *did* matter to her anymore was having sex with her boyfriend. Her boyfriend who had punched Greg in the face.

Reliving that memory might never get old.

Regardless, there was no convincing left to do on Chris's part.

And now the past fifteen minutes had been spent making out in the front seat of his F-350. There hadn't been any conversation on the way over from prom, but both seemed okay with it. For Jessica's part, she knew from ample experience that the only thing one *could* do after something like that was to push it to the back of the brain.

As the cheerleading squad was so fond of saying during the football games, *Push it back! Push it back! Waaaay back.* Jess adopted that as her mantra for the evening.

There had been a few moments where Chris's shift of body language indicated that he was about to say something, but for whatever reason, sound never broke the barrier of his lips.

The making out had seemed like the best way to transition from an uncomfortable silence to sex, so Jessica had, perhaps too aggressively, lunged at Chris as soon as the engine was off. He hadn't appeared to mind.

He presently pulled away and made a T with his hands. "Time out. One second." He jumped out of the truck, grabbed something from the back seat and then headed toward the back bumper. A moment later Jess heard a strange sound and turned to see that Chris was inflating an air mattress in the truck bed. That was thoughtful, at least. She'd wondered about the comfort level of sex on the hard, uneven metal, what with the thrusting she assumed would be involved.

He disappeared and then reappeared at her door, which he opened before offering her a hand down. She'd long since kicked off her wedge shoes and didn't need the assistance, even with her dress making it difficult to spread her knees more than two feet apart, but she accepted the help all the same. It was what Destinee had explained (in depth) was considered foreplay—where a man was really nice and considerate for a short amount of time leading into sex—and had insisted it was important for women to take that where they could get it. At first, Jessica found the idea of foreplay unappealing and embarrassing, until she realized that there were plenty of other animals who practiced it—lions, bats, monkeys, to name a few.

Surprisingly, that helped her warm up to it rather than intensifying her aversion. She hoped he didn't try to perform oral sex on her, though, like male bats sometimes did to female bats. That seemed a little intense, or maybe she just wasn't huge on bats. Plus, she'd never come to a definite conclusion or taken action regarding the pubic hair dilemma. Sure, she'd shaved it all off once, but the days of maddening itching that followed as she tried to do basic things like sit, walk, and pleasure herself made the whole thing not worth it. That didn't mean she wasn't still self-conscious about it, though; it just meant she hadn't decided what to do.

The battery-powered air pump had done its job to

completion by the time they stood next to the rear bumper of the truck, and Chris made quick work of shutting off the pump and plugging up the air flow before he helped Jessica onto their sex pallet. She leaned back on her elbows and stared up into the night sky as she waited for Chris to climb on.

Her mind wandered back to the last time she'd given the stars any thought. It'd been in the back of Greg's El Camino, and she'd been high as a kite. She wondered if Chris cared about stars.

"You want a Lone Star?" he asked.

That counted. "Yep."

He climbed up in the truck bed carrying two ice-cold tall boys. He handed one to Jessica, but not before doing her the favor of opening it.

More foreplay.

"How you feeling?" he asked.

She shrugged. "Fine, I guess."

"What happened in the gym. You wanna talk about it?"

"Probably best if we don't." She took a long swig.

"Yeah, that sounds good. Let's talk about it tomorrow. Or next week."

"Or never," she offered. "We could talk about it never and that would probably be okay."

Chris rubbed at the back of his neck. "Yeah, I don't really know what I'd say about it anyway."

"Exactly."

He lay on his back next to her and stared up at the sky. "Did you know there's an infinite number of ways to connect the stars so that they form the shape of a dick?"

She hadn't thought of the universe in those terms. "I didn't."

"It's true."

She knew that, too, was merely foreplay, but she took a sip of her Lone Star and tried her hand at tracing the lines between stars to make a dick shape anyway. Out here, away from all the light pollution, with so many stars to choose from, she couldn't technically *disprove* Chris's theory.

He rolled onto his side, the movement on the air mattress jostling her abruptly, and faced her. She turned toward him, too, with only a little bit of difficulty.

"I love you," he said.

"I love you too." This time it didn't feel so foreign. Was saying "I love you" foreplay, too? It sort of felt like it. Saying it had certainly intensified her desire to have sex with him.

"Sometimes I don't feel worthy of you."

That definitely *didn't* feel like foreplay. "That's dumb. You're nicer to me than any guy I know."

He leaned in and kissed her and it tasted like Lone Star and lust.

He pulled back just enough to speak. "God, Jess, I've wanted this for so long. Are you sure God's cool with it?"

"Yeah."

"Did you talk with Him about it?"

"Of course," she lied.

He nodded. "And are *you* ready?"

She was more than ready. But she didn't think saying, "Yeah, let's get this over with already," was great foreplay, so she simply nodded.

"You're not gonna …"

"No."

He set his jaw and nodded then placed his can on the side of the truck, stripped off his tuxedo jacket, and began unbuttoning his shirt. She realized she'd never even seen his shirt off in a sexual context before, and her mind flashed back to the Steps of Intimacy handout they'd been given at the start of sex ed all those year ago. Shirt off was step six or seven. Sex was step eighteen. They were skipping some serious steps, and Jess wondered if maybe they should just ease into it with what her mother called a "good old-fashioned handsy." Maybe she could mix that in.

Chris stared at her expectantly. *I guess it's my turn.*

But the only thing she had to take off was her entire dress. Well, it would happen eventually. She set her can on the side of the truck and reached behind her, trying to find the zipper.

"Here," Chris said, and rolled her over so her back was to him. Slowly he unzipped the dress, and she felt her lower abs clench in a not entirely unpleasant way. She sat up, and he ran his hands down her back before slipping the dress off her shoulders and inhaling deeply. "You're so beautiful, Jessica."

She could feel her cheeks redden and wished he'd stop talking and start fucking already. She wanted to get this over with, not because she didn't want it, but because she wanted to work out all the kinks and get onto to the good stuff people talked about.

Every time anyone she knew mentioned sex, it amounted to the same thing: the first time was a disaster, but after that it started to get awesome. It was time to rip off the Band-Aid.

She shimmied the dress off the rest of the way so she was in the strapless bra and thong her mother had insisted was necessary for a dress that tight, and turned to face Chris, who sucked in air sharply as he drank in the sight of her body.

She nodded at him. "Take off your pants." Eh, not quite the seductive tone she'd wanted, but it seemed to excite him anyway. Maybe foreplay for guys was different from foreplay for girls.

He hopped to quickly, fumbling briefly over his belt before he mastered it and slid off his dress pants, leaving him in only his boxer briefs, which were jammed packed with that dragon she'd spent the past two years fearing but knew she would someday have to slay.

Time to unleash the beast.

He ran his hands down her bare skin, like he couldn't believe it was real. Then he reached behind him without turning his head, grabbed his Lone Star, and took a long sip of it.

What was the correct exit point of the briefs? She'd never considered it, but now that she was here, she wasn't sure if etiquette dictated that she pull him free through the opening in the front or over the waistband. Was there a guide for this? They certainly didn't cover it in sex ed.

She opted for the opening in the front, and as the rest of Chris collapsed onto the air mattress like a limp rag the moment her hand made contact with him, she assumed he didn't mind the choice she'd made.

It's a Miracle!

Shit. What do I even do with this?

She flopped it around in her hand a little bit. It was completely unwieldy.

Is this a both-hand kind of thing? She rubbed it in between her palms, then realize she was essentially giving him an Indian rug burn and stopped immediately.

What would porn do?

She was spared the effort, though, as he couldn't wait any longer and pushed himself up so that he was positioned above her as she lay on her back.

He slid down his boxers and looked into her eyes. "Are you sure you're ready?"

"Yes." *God, can we get this over with and move on to the good stuff?*

"You can say no at any time, and I'll stop."

She nodded. "I know."

But he still seemed unsure. "Good. Because, seriously, you have to let me know. I don't want to be, you know, smote."

"You're good. Can we just get to it?"

"Yes. Yeah. Of course." He slid her underwear down, and she gritted her teeth, bracing for judgement at what he saw, but it didn't come.

He paused again, hovering just before the point of no return, and looked into her eyes again. "Still good?"

"Yep." Then she remembered. "Wait, no!"

"Huh?"

"Condom."

"Oh right."

His briefs reminded her of a circus tent as he pulled

them back up, hopped out of the truck, grabbed her clutch from the cab, then climbed back on top. He struggled to open a condom and, when it was clear he didn't know how to use it, she said, "Here. I learned about this," and put it on for him.

"Uh, thanks," he said before resuming the position. "So, uh, here we go."

She closed her eyes, thinking that was the decorous thing to do, but when he shifted his hips forward, she wondered what had gone wrong and opened her eyes to look up at him. He seemed to be wondering the same thing.

"What—" she began, not wanting to get into the specifics.

"I don't know. That was ... sudden. Maybe I'm just nervous." He put on his game face, the one he reserved, literally, for games, and sucked in air. "Let me try again."

"Okay ..."

She didn't want to look down her body at the actual malfunctioning part, so instead she shut her eyes.

And again, it felt like someone was mushing a warm stress ball between her legs.

"Dammit!" he yelled.

IT'S A MIRACLE!

"Fucking shit!" she yelled louder.

Why ... just why?

PLEASE. YOU THINK I'D LET MY DAUGHTER ENGAGE IN SEX BEFORE MARRIAGE?

You mean like you did? Like my mom did? Like Mary did?

NOT THE SAME.

"Arrrrrrrrg!"

Chris had leapt off her after the first outburst, leaving her flailing in frustration on her back atop the air mattress, which squeaked and squelched beneath her.

"I hate you, God!" she screamed, pointing upward at the universe for lack of a more accurate physical location. "I hate you!"

LISTEN, NO ONE EVER SAID LIFE WOULD BE EASY.

She let her arms flop down to her side and shut her eyes to tamp down the rage. *Push it back! Push it back! Waaay back!*

Please, lord God, just let me have sex. Amen.

ARE YOU TRYING TO PRAY YOUR WAY OUT OF THIS?

Is it working?

NOPE.

She sighed and opened her eyes to find Chris staring at her wide-eyed, his briefs still tented, despite his inability to perform when push came to shove, literally.

She propped herself up onto her elbows and frowned. "Don't take it personally," she said. "It's not you; it's me."

End of Book 3, *It's a Miracle!*

* * *

Keep reading for a sneak peek of book 4 and a howdy from the author →

Like free stuff?

Get a free e-book copy of the quirky satire
Wimbledon, Kentucky

Go to
BookHip.com/CDMRGL
to claim yours!

Bonus: Nu Alpha Omega

18 AGC

Jessica had hoped that in graduating high school and moving out on her own, she'd also graduate from plastic-covered furniture. But as she plopped down on her extra-long twin mattress for the first time and felt the stiff crackle of fresh polyurethane underneath her, she knew it was one of the necessary evils of dorm life. Brand-new sheets would come later, but for now she was still surrounded by bags of unpacked Walmart essentials and Destinee and Rex were still lingering around in the tiny space—Destinee worrying her lip as she ran her hand over various surfaces, inspecting who knew what quality and continually finding it wanting and Rex gazing reverently around at the stock furnishings, misty-eyed.

"Best days of my life," he said, like Jessica was supposed to understand. But then he pulled back from his reverie and looked directly at her. "Now remember what I told you,

Jess. It could be the best four years of your life or the best one year of your life. All depends on the decisions you make."

During down months between her final day at Mooremont High and move-in day at Texas State University, Rex had spent so much time at the McCloud home, eating almost every meal there and staying over every single night, that Jessica wasn't sure if he technically lived there or not. At some point during those long, long, *long* days, Rex had apparently decided to step into the father roll (whether she liked it or not). But as far as Jess was concerned, there wasn't much point to developing new habits this close to moving away, other than one: learning how to ignore Rex's fatherly advice.

"You're here to learn," he continued, leaning back against the rickety dresser. "You forget that, your grades slip, you party too hard, get ..."

Jess spared him saying the word. "Get pregnant?"

Rex nodded.

Destinee wrapped up her inspection of the body-length mirror and smacked Rex on the arm with the back of her hand. "Please. You think I'd raise a child who didn't know how to use a damn condom?"

Jessica sighed, wishing she had occasion to ever use a condom, mostly for Chris's sake. They'd decided immediately and unanimously that no one else needed to know about their little sex problem, and when Jessica had returned home the morning after prom looking freshly manhandled, Destinee had practically thrown a party in her honor, assuming what any good parent would.

"I mean," Rex said cautiously, "there are other ways to get pregnant than sex." He raised his brows significantly.

Both Destinee and Jess narrowed their eyes at him. What exactly was he implying?

"You mean immaculate conception?" Jess asked.

Rex shrugged minutely, "It's happened before, is all I'm saying …"

Jess gagged. "You know he's my dad, right? I mean you realize this, right? He's not going to get me pregnant."

"And we already been over this," Destinee added. "It wasn't rape. I was beyond willing."

"You know," Jess said, jumping in, "I really need to unpack and get settled in and check in with Chris."

"Right," Destinee said, staying planted where she stood. "You know when the roommate is coming back? I'd like to meet her."

Jess shrugged. Half of the room had already been set up, the bed made, the walls decorated in a celebrity crush collage that Jess might have appreciated, could her gaze have done anything but home in on the stunning grin and hazel eyes of Jameson Fractal staring back at her from the center of the hodgepodge. The girl's comforter had big yellow and pink flowers that felt like a congenial assault on Jessica's retinas. In short, it seemed like her roommate was what everyone thought freshman girls should be.

"You can meet her next time you visit," Jess said. It would be a while till Destinee made the drive down to San Marcos again, but the suggestion that she *would* at some point in the future would suffice to get her moving out the door.

Jessica rode the elevator back up after a quick good-bye to Destinee and a few more words of wisdom from Rex. ("Trashcan punch may sound like a good time, but it's roofie central, got that?" Coincidentally, Jessica's imagination couldn't concoct a scenario where "trashcan" in the description of anything would make her want to put it in her mouth.)

A strange feeling came over her as she ascended. It was unlike any she'd ever experienced. She tried to name it, and it wasn't until the elevator doors opened and she stepped into the empty hallway that she realized what it was. She was *unattached*. Untethered. Separate. An individual. She held out her arms and looked at them. She was a separate entity from everything else. She could spend the day wandering through the woods and no one would be affected, no one would have to know. Her time was unaccounted for. She stood in the hallway, blinking for a solid thirty seconds before a vibration in her back pocket rattled her ass cheek and snapped her out of her revelation.

It was Chris. She read the text. *"Training running long. Won't make it to lunch. Love you."*

She headed toward her room as she texted him back not to worry and didn't notice that another human being was occupying the space, sitting quietly with her hands folded in her lap, until Jessica had already made it back to her bed and flopped onto it with a *crackle-swish*.

"Oh hi," Jess said, smiling at her new roommate.

"Jessica McCloud," the girl breathed, her big round eyes open wide above a small turned up nose. "I'm Leslie. I'm your new roommate." She jumped up and held out her hand.

Shaking seemed a little formal for someone Jessica was sure to see naked and hear poop in the near future, but she didn't want to be rude, so she shook.

When Leslie returned to sitting on her bed, pulling her feet up underneath her butt, there was no sound of fresh plastic. "I just have to say, when I got the email about who my new roommate would be, and I saw your name, I almost didn't believe it. I mean, I'd heard you were coming to Texas State, but I thought maybe I'd bump into you on campus once or twice and you wouldn't know who I was. But now we're roommates! And you already know my name."

Jess tried to remember Leslie's last name from the email she'd received about her over the summer but couldn't. Bucky? No, that wasn't a last name. Why did she keep thinking it was Bucky, though? Maybe it *was* Bucky. Leslie Bucky? No one in their right mind would give a child that name.

"Do you want to go get lunch?" Leslie continued, grinning. Then she froze as if she'd just remembered. "Oh, you probably already have plans."

Jessica had never been one to care much about hairstyles, but she had a sudden urge to braid Leslie's hair. It wasn't an urge born out of friendship or really anything positive. It was rooted in the fact that Leslie's hair was the dullest shade of dark brown Jessica had ever seen (not that her own ash brown hair provided much to write home about) and was such a frizz ball, despite somehow also being thin, that it made Jess both uncomfortable and agitated to look at. Really? Your first day on campus and you don't even bother to manage your hair?

What was she asking? Oh right. "Yeah, I'm meeting up with my boyfriend for lunch in a bit," she lied.

Leslie grinned and nodded slowly. "Right. He's here too. I bet y'all are happy you get to stay together."

"Yeah."

"You think you'll get married?"

"What?"

Leslie gasped. "I'm so sorry! I'm prying! Oh my God I —" She gasped again and covered her mouth with a flap palm.

Who the hell is this girl?

"What is it?"

"I'm sorry," Leslie said, and it sounded like she meant it.

"For what?"

"For saying the ... the G word."

Jess tried to think of a dirty word that started with G, but couldn't come up with anything. Gook? That was supposed to be bad. But she was pretty sure Leslie hadn't said gook. She shook her head vaguely.

"G-O-D," Leslie whispered.

"Oh. God. That's not a bad word, Leslie. He doesn't care if you use his name."

Leslie shifted so her knees were pulled up to her chest. "So it's true. He's really ... you're His ..."

"Yep." Jessica knew this would be a thing. She'd done her best to mentally prepare for it, too. A new city with all new people had its strong appeal, but it also meant conversations like this by the boatful. Leslie could prove good practice for those who weren't as eager to hear what she had to say.

"Wow. So you can speak to Him?"

"Yep."

Leslie ducked her head down as she whispered, "Is He here right now?"

"Yes and no," Jess replied at full volume. "But there's also no point in whispering."

"Ah, okay." Leslie smiled placidly and nodded, though an unfocused look in her eyes hinted that she might not completely understand. "So you can really do all those miracles? The field goals and the resurrections—"

"Yeah, but I don't do either of those anymore."

"Right, right. I saw your tweets about it. But I mean"—she leaned forward—"do you still bring people back to life sometimes? You know, privately?"

"No," Jess said plainly. "I don't do it publicly or privately. I thought that was pretty clear."

The girl shrugged. "Well sure, but you never know. I just thought I'd ask."

You and everyone else.

She tried not to think about all tweets along the lines of:

> *.@therealmccloud if u dont wanna tell every1 just DM me the truth*

> .@therealmccloud *we all know u brought back jamaal lewis after that car accident quit playin*
>
> .@therealmccloud *I DM u sumthin u gon like ;-) all 9in of it B=====D*

"Yep. Definitely gave up those miracles completely."

"Well, I guess you did go out with a bang. I mean, if you're going to stop, you might as well make the last one count."

What was she ...? Oh right. Jimmy's faked resurrection in White Light Church. People thought she'd done that. And people thought she liked him. And *people liked him.*

It was the last bit that boggled her mind the most. She understood people *wanting* to like Jimmy. Hell, she still wanted to like him. But wanting to like someone and actually being able to stomach a person weren't always the same thing.

"Are you sure you can't get lunch?"

Jess smiled apologetically. "I really can't. I need to get some of this stuff in order before I meet up with Chris."

Leslie jumped up. "Can I help at all?"

One task jumped to mind immediately, like it'd been spring loaded in Jessica's subconscious waiting for the perfect moment to launch forward. "Yes. Could you do me a favor and just take down that photo of Jameson Fractal?"

It was clearly not what the girl had been expecting, and the deviation caused her pause before a light went on behind her dulled eyes. "Oh. Oh! Yes. Yes, I'm so sorry. I'm an idiot. I should have known ..."

"No, no," Jess assured her half-heartedly. "It's fine."

Leslie hastily ripped his face off of her collage before turning back toward Jess. "Anyone else? Gavin? Garth? Paul? Liam?"

Jessica scanned the collage more closely. She spotted another unwelcome face that wasn't quite as carved into her psyche as Jameson's but had to go for what she felt was an equally valid reason. "Is that Ross Hawthorn?" She only recognized him from the old, faded T-shirt Destinee still wore to bed on occasion with the singer's likeness plastered across the front. Seeing her mother casually sport the face of the man who God had impersonated to knock her up left Jessica deeply disconcerted without fail. Avoiding those unwelcome encounters with that T-shirt had been one of the things she'd looked forward to when she moved away, actually. And now here he was again, grinning back at her, hot as ever, which Jessica found as uncomfortable as ever.

Leslie scrunched up her nose. "Yeah. Is he not allowed either?"

Jess shook her head. "No, he's definitely not allowed."

Leslie reached up and grabbed the cutout of his face. "Can I ask why?"

"I'd rather you didn't."

She ripped Ross off the wall. "Okay, anything else?"

"No, that's all. Thanks Leslie. Let me know how the dining hall food is." Giving the girl a job seemed like a good idea. Jessica knew it to be the best way to calm the nerves of domesticated dogs, and Leslie seemed closer to that than to a functioning human being.

"Will do!" She grabbed her wallet, with her student ID proudly displayed behind a soft plastic window, and her key fob, with more keys and dangling keychains than any eighteen-year-old should need.

Jess fell backward onto her undressed bed as soon as she was alone again and held her phone up above her face, pulling up her ongoing message with her best friend.

She texted: *Just met the new roommate. Call me when you can. You won't believe it.*

She waited for a response, and after two minutes figured she could probably find a better use of her time than staring at the wall where the previous tenant had used a tack to poke holes in the shape of a stubby penis. The dick pointed diagonally up toward a smoke detector that hung out of its dock in the ceiling and beeped red, presumably to alert those who might see it that everything was just A-OK!

It was too silent to set up her room. She was sure the quiet wouldn't last long; she'd been told she was one of the only freshmen in her dorm, so once the sophomores and juniors moved in a couple days later, she might miss the silence. But for now, it just took the amazing feeling of being on her own and put a sour spin on it.

She pulled her remote from the clear plastic tub where she'd packed it away and plugged in the TV. The first channel was fuzz, so she scanned until she found the local stations. Without cable, there'd be no Animal Planet, but maybe that was for the best. She could avoid the temptation of staying in her room all day. A blurb for the evening news came on. It might not be a bad idea to get a feel for what happened in Central Texas. It couldn't be any more boring than what happened in West Texas.

"The governor's race heats up as Texas Attorney General Grant investigates both candidates on charges of bribery, libel, and misappropriation of funds. More sunshine in the forecast this week, and beginning tonight, our six-part special: you trust the water you drink, clean your food with, and bathe your children in to be safe, but do you really know what you're pouring over your skin and putting in your body? New shocking details about what's in our water supply may have you considering alternatives to tap-water bathing. And lastly, we check in with our affiliate out of Odessa for a shocking update about Texas's most well-known reverend."

A picture of Jimmy was only on the screen for half a second before Jess shut off the TV. She remained staring at the black set, though, letting this new information set in. Not the aquaphobia, but the more important bit: She was four hours from home, and it still wasn't far enough away to forget about Jimmy. Reverend Dean mania wasn't a localized sickness. That was unfortunate. Maybe she'd brought it with her to central Texas. Who was she kidding? Of course she did. She was patient zero in that regard. A Jimmy-shaped cloud hovered over her wherever she went, now that he'd so firmly established himself in the public eye as her caretaker and she his divine ward.

A peach pit of loneliness that had been waiting dormant in her chest began to dissolve into her blood stream and spread throughout the rest of her. She supposed people made friends when they were lonely, but she'd never learned how to do that. All her relationships—both good and bad—had been forged as a result of the pressure-cooker of a tiny town she'd grown up in. Force two people to be in close proximity long enough and they bond in one way or another. But that wasn't the set-up at a school with tens of thousands of students. The only person in close proximity would be Leslie, and Jessica hoped to avoid too much on the bonding front with that one.

God? You there?

Nothing.

Well shit, she really was alone.

She pulled out the old Dell laptop Destinee and Coach Rex had given to her the week before and started it up. She needed someone to talk to, and she already knew who it would be, who would listen to her woes, provide reassurance, and not overreact to Jessica's complaints.

She pulled up her email and began typing in the address *dthomas@*

Her computer did the rest, and she moved to the subject line: *Made it!*

She rolled her shoulders to release the tension, and then let herself be honest. Her former teacher would understand.

Want to keep reading? The rest of *Nu Alpha Omega* is just a few clicks away.

Get yours at:
bit.ly/JCbook4

About the Author

H. CLAIRE TAYLOR has lived in Austin since the eighties (it's her hometown) and hasn't yet found a compelling reason to move away.

After being a Very Good Student™ of creative writing at Texas State University, she worked an assortment of unfulfilling jobs until her inner tortured artist could recover from four soul-crushing years of academia, at which point she held her nose and jumped into the muddy waters of writing comedy full time.

Now she shares a home with her husband and two black-and-white mutts and suffers from an unhealthy dependency on Post-It Notes that she can quit whenever she wants. Really.

When she's not working on her novels, she's blogging (www.hclaireblogs.com) and recording her comedy podcast, *Something Nice to Say,* which you can subscribe to on iTunes for free.

Casually stalk her:
www.hclairetaylor.com

Also by H. Claire Taylor

The Jessica Christ Series
The Beginning (Book 1)
A Great Gulf (short story)
And It Was Good (Book 2)
It's a Miracle! (Book 3)
Nu Alpha Omega (Book 4)
It is Risen (Book 5)

Kilhaven Police (w/Brock Bloodworth)
Shift Work (Book 1)

Wimbledon, Kentucky
A Single's Guide to Texas Roadways

All titles can be found at
www.amazon.com/author/hclairetaylor

www.ingramcontent.com/pod-product-compliance
Lightning Source LLC
LaVergne TN
LVHW051544070426
835507LV00021B/2398